About the Author

Bill Adams is an Englishman married to an Indian educationalist. After leaving school at 16 and unloading lorries for a time, he went to night school and then won a scholarship to university. Following a postgraduate diploma at Oxford University he lectured in Communications, wrote radio scripts, formed a theatre company – and now lives in New Delhi where he runs training courses for computer software companies, heads a Soccer Academy and writes regularly for newspapers of the Indian sub continent.

The Five Lessons of Life

Bill Adams

RIDER

LONDON · SYDNEY · AUCKLAND · JOHANNESBURG

First published in 2000

3 5 7 9 10 8 6 4

Published in 2000 by Rider,
an imprint of Ebury Press, Random House,
20 Vauxhall Bridge Road, London SW1V 2SA
www.randomhouse.co.uk

Random House Australia (Pty) Limited
20 Alfred Street, Milsons Point, Sydney,
New South Wales 2061, Australia

Random House New Zealand Limited
18 Poland Road, Glenfield,
Auckland 10, New Zealand

Random House South Africa (Pty) Limited
Endulini, 5A Jubilee Road,
Parktown 2193, South Africa

The Random House Group Limited Reg. No. 954009

Papers used by Rider are natural, recyclable products made from wood grown in
sustainable forests.

Typeset by SX Composing DTP, Rayleigh, Essex
Printed and bound in Great Britain by Biddles Ltd, Guildford and King's Lynn

A CIP catalogue record for this book is available from the British Library

ISBN 0-7126-7075-0

Contents

Preface

This book records the teachings of Sangratan, a healer/ counsellor who travels the passes of the Himalayas near the Indo-Tibet border. It sets out the Five Lessons of Life familiar to the mountain people who live there, lessons which have helped them to cope with the harsh climatic conditions of the region as well as with those problems common to people everywhere; lessons that can help us all cope with life's problems, whatever our situation or background.

This book is written as a guide for those who want to take control of their lives and its message is for everyone seeking to improve the quality of their lives.

It also records my meetings with Sangratan and in the process it documents aspects of the lifestyle of the polyandrous tribal people among whom he lives and travels. Though he claims no special mystical powers, it is obvious to those who have met him that he is not like other men, not least because he has a remarkable ability to turn up when he is most needed, and seems to be aware of what you are thinking even before you do yourself.

The Five Lessons are particularly useful for those who find it difficult to cope when faced with problems or to approach them objectively. So often, highly competent people who excel at the most demanding and high-pressured jobs find that they are making a mess of their emotional and/or social lives. The teachings of Sangratan show how, by investigating our personal needs and by applying the approach that he sets out, we can lead more satisfying and productive lives in every sphere.

Unlike other self-help books, this one does not require you to search the depths of your psyche to find inner strength, meaning or power. The premise on which this book is based is quite straightforward. It is that many of us have lost our direction and, in spite of our relative prosperity (compared with those in the 'Third World'), if we wish to be happy and fulfilled we need to follow an approach to living that western societies have by and large lost, but which has blossomed and developed in the valleys of the Himalayas.

This book is *your* guide. It allows you to concentrate only on those aspects of your life that you decide to look at and will help you find answers to the questions which will shape the best possible life for you. It is especially helpful for people who are having difficulty knowing exactly what they want out of life. To use the American jargon, this book helps you to 'get focused and keep focused'.

The Five Lessons of Life have their origins in the world's most ancient religions but this is not a book about religion; it is simply a practical guide to improving your life. It shows you how to approach it in the best way possible and also shows you what to do when your efforts are blocked and problems arise. In Appendix I, I have set out the essence of each lesson and how to apply it.

The teachings of Sangratan are both simple and philosophically powerful. In writing this book I have been conscious of my obligation to make them as accessible as I can. If you fail to gain help and guidance from this book, the fault is mine. If these teachings change your life for the better (as they have mine), the credit goes to a wonderful man who has spent his life wandering the valleys of the Himalayas: Sangratan the Amchi.

Introduction

In the north Indian state of Himachal Pradesh, high in the Himalayas, lies the district of Kinnuer. It is an ancient land, steeped in myth and legend. The lower slopes of the mountains are covered in pine forests which are home to an abundance of wild life. On these mountains reside leopards and other predators, along with a host of other animals and birds. It is home to the Kinnars, a tribal people whose polyandrous way of life has survived little changed throughout the centuries.* They are a people who have learnt to live in harmony with their beautiful but difficult environment, and with each other.

Kinnuer has a special place in the history of India and Hinduism. The most ancient Hindu texts mention many of the places in this area, and it is in the mountains of this region that Shiva and a host of Hindu gods and goddesses are said to have resided and performed some of their most remarkable exploits.

In ancient days Kinnuer was also the home of the Pandavs, the ancient rulers of India, and the protagonists of the most famous Hindu religious epic, *The Mahabharata*. The King of the Pandavs and his brothers, the *Mahabharata* recounts, all marry the same woman, Draupadi, and this form of polyandry is still practised today by the inhabitants of the area.

Until 1993 entry to Kinnuer was highly restricted. The

---

* In its pure form, polyandry works as follows. The eldest son will be married off; the second will share his marital rights. The fourth and subsequent sons *may* enter into this arrangement, but are more likely to be encouraged to marry the eldest daughter of a family with no sons. The other daughters of the family may be allowed to share this man but are more likely to be married off. The third son is usually given to a monastery to be raised as a monk or *lama*.

area was closed to foreign nationals, and Indians needed a hard-to-obtain permit from the Indian government. Even today the heavy snowfalls of winter and the flash floods of the monsoons make the area inaccessible for much of the year. The snows close the passes in and out of the region from October until May, and the monsoon swells the rivers in July to a point where bridges become dangerous to use, and are sometimes simply swept away. Under these circumstances the unique lifestyle of these tribal people has been protected, and it still flourishes.

Every successful society has a common philosophy of life and shared values. Underpinning the societies of the West we have the state and a formal system of written laws and regulations. Underpinning the society of the Kinnar are the Lessons of Life – a practical philosophy of self-respect and interdependence, rationality and reverence; acceptance of what is, and the pursuit of what can be.

Each Kinnar child learns the Lessons of Life informally throughout childhood, and the close-knit nature of the family and the tribe ensure that there is a commonality of approach to problems. However, sometimes in the isolation of their farmhouses, people can feel overwhelmed by events, or relationships may come under strain. At times such as these, even the most practical people need advice, counselling, or simply someone outside the family to share their troubles with. At such times, many people turn to Sangratan the Amchi.*

* Amchi are travelling healers who practise a combination of Buddhist and Ayurvedic medicine and can be found throughout Tibet and the adjoining parts of India. It is said that Buddha was the first Amchi.

Sangratan travels from farm to farm dispensing his medicines and knowledge, curing the sick, and counselling the poor of spirit. He is revered as a great healer, a wise counsellor and a man of extraordinary powers. He is all of these things. Most importantly, he is enlightened by the Lessons of Life, a simple yet powerful set of guidelines designed to help each person discover and effectively pursue that which is most important to them. In part, the Lessons of Life as they exist today are Sangratan's creation, for he has compiled them from several ancient texts which are concerned with living life to obtain the optimum amount of joy.

The Lessons of Life are important to the tribal people of the Himalayas in their struggle to prosper in harsh, isolated conditions, but they are also important to all of us. In the modern world, with its isolations, stresses and tensions, outside pressures often cause us to drift away from what we really want, from what makes us happy. We lose ourselves in our work, or in our relationships, not realising that we have isolated ourselves from what we really want. We know we are unhappy but often we do not realise how much we have denied our true selves, for the sake of our careers, for a particular relationship, or simply for a 'quiet life'. Many of us wake up one morning to find that chances have gone by, and opportunities have been missed. Sometimes we feel helpless and frustrated. Sometimes we feel isolated or that life is passing us by and we are merely existing, while happiness and joy are for others. Though we enjoy the benefits of modern society which are denied to many in the 'developing' countries, we sometimes feel that if we obtained more we would somehow be happier, more fulfilled.

Sangratan's teachings, as encapsulated in the Lessons of Life, show that each of us can find fulfilment by looking within ourselves, discovering who we really are and what we really want. While recognising that each of us needs varying degrees of solitude and sociability, the Lessons of Life are based on the simple premise that we are basically social creatures who need to be emotionally close to others. To achieve this, we need to learn how to live in harmony with ourselves and with others.

The Lessons of Life also recognise that everything changes, and coping with change is often hard. Children who only yesterday needed our every attention now have their own lives, their own friends, their own paths to follow. Nothing has a physical permanence: buildings decay and require repair, refurbishment or replacement; towns, cities, entire civilisations come into being, change and often disappear. Our bodies change from childhood to adolescence, adolescence to young adulthood. We change when we become parents, as we age and become more frail. We change when we have new experiences, learn new things, see events from different perspectives. We change when we lose something or someone dear to us. We change when we acquire something wonderful. We change a little bit every day. The Lessons of Life recognise the change life brings and show us how we can keep sight of who we really are, and what we really want. They also recognise that most of the important things in life require effort and commitment. We 'make' friends, 'earn' respect, 'achieve' success, 'find' love.

Even in the most contented of lives, as things change, problems arise. Some people who cope very well when life is on an even keel cannot handle change and problems. This is particularly true in traditional societies like that of the Kinnars. The Lessons of Life have helped many who, because of some natural or personal change, have been faced with an unfamiliar set of circumstances.

In modern western societies which are subject to almost continuous change, problems associated with personal instability are much more common. In a fast-changing world it is vital to learn the Lessons of Life, for they help us to think clearly about our problems and how to approach them so that they can be resolved in the most effective way possible.

Specifically, the Lessons of Life guide us and help us find answers to the questions which will provide us with the best possible life. They encapsulate an approach to living which can help everyone become more effective in everything they do.

Sangratan asks: 'Without knowing ourselves, how can we know others?' The Lessons of Life show us how to know ourselves better, to determine and prioritise our values so that we know exactly what is important to us. They show us how to set about fulfilling our needs, so that we can work towards steadily improving our lives. They show us how to save time and energy when pursuing what we decide is important and how to review our progress.

They also guide us in our relationships with others. Sangratan explains that it is our relationships with others that bring us either real happiness or sorrow. Living harmoniously with the people around us is the source of joy; to thrive we all require a degree of closeness and harmony with our relatives and friends.

The Five Lessons of Life as set out in this book are the

essence of Sangratan's teachings but they are not the essence of the man. He is remarkable in many ways, and surprisingly for one whose teachings are based on the need to live in harmony with others, his lifestyle sets him apart. There is no doubt that he is not like other men, and that all who have met him, love him for his warmth, kindness and concern. However, he walks through life accompanied only by Kirti, a dog who is his constant companion. Sangratan claims that they have been together in many forms through many lives, and will be for many more.

In this book I have tried to include all I know about Sangratan, for I believe that you cannot divorce the teacher from his teachings. Little is known of his past, for he is not concerned with it. He says: 'The past shapes us, and then we shape and reshape the past . . . when we look back at the past we must always remember that we have given that time its shape.'

Sangratan learned his healing in Tibet and from the Ayurveds of the Indian Himalayas. He said that he always winters in Tibet, where he makes his own remedies and stocks up on the medicines produced by the Buddhist monks. For his Ayurvedic remedies he collects herbs from the forest.

During the course of our meetings Sangratan made several predictions concerning floods, droughts and large-scale violence. A number of these predicted events will, according to Sangratan, take place in Northern India in the next ten years but some are of worldwide significance. I have included them in Appendix III so that you can judge for yourself the remarkable nature of this wonderful man.

I

• •

Sangratan the Amchi

On the road above Kalpa there is an old wood mill. A diesel-driven saw roughly shapes the trunks of pine trees into beams capable of holding a stone-clad roof and several hundredweight of snow. Small men carry large beams of wood across their shoulders from this mill to whoever needs them. The beams are between three and four metres long and eight to twelve inches square. The men are bent almost double with the weight. They shuffle along the steep mountain track and those they meet step aside as they struggle along in the thin air and high summer temperatures. At the moment of passing they look up with a broad smile of greeting on their faces. In a land of extreme hardship, they have learnt how to be happy.

That fateful summer of 1994 I walked the road above Kalpa with my wife Abha and our nine-year-old son Sean. We stepped to the side to let the beam-carriers pass, marvelling at their strength, tenacity and good humour. For them life was very hard; for us it was easy. We were on vacation, staying at the farmhouse of a wealthy landowner, enjoying the awe-inspiring scenery, the clean mountain air and the respite from the 50 degrees Celsius temperatures of Delhi, enjoying the peace and tranquillity.

We had married in England in 1983. Abha had taken a sabbatical from her job as a lecturer in English Literature at the University of Delhi to do an M.Phil in Drama, at Leeds University, and we met at her first production. Within days of our meeting I was in love with this kind, intelligent, beautiful Indian woman. We spent most of our early married life in Leeds, where Abha worked for the BBC and I managed a Social Work project and ran training courses for public service workers. In 1992 we moved to Delhi to be with Abha's aging mother and give Sean an Indian childhood. Two years of readjustment followed. Two years of getting used to power shortages, water shortages, and the frustrations imposed by the antiquated Indian Bureaucracy. Two years of hard work re-establishing ourselves as successful professionals; Abha, as a prominent educationalist and I as a Corporate Communications trainer for multinational companies. We needed this holiday to recharge our batteries, to get away from Delhi and to explore and understand another facet of the wonderful culture of India.

On this particular day we were walking along the mountain track from Kalpa to Rogi, and planned to have a picnic. The track clung to the side of the mountain and twisted and turned with every nuance of the terrain. Below us mountain eagles glided silently, searching for prey in the nooks and crevices of the valley floor. To our left we could look down 2,000 feet to the floor of the valley and the mighty Sutlej river churning its way towards the plains of Northern India, hundreds of kilometres away. Above us, on the other side of the valley, the snow-covered peaks of the Kinnuer Kailash glistened in the late morning sun, seeming so close that we felt we could reach out and touch them.

Halfway to Rogi a mountain stream had cut a tributary valley into the steep mountain side, and here, where the stream bisected the track, we sat, drank the cool clean water and rested in the shade of a rocky outcrop. The afternoon sun and our exertions in the thin air had tired us, and we stretched out sleepily after eating the snack which was our lunch for that day. Five more kilometres to Rogi – and all uphill!

Too soon the lengthening shadows told us that it was time to move on, and, somewhat reluctantly, we gathered up our knapsacks, took one final drink of the clear mountain water and started off up the track. We hadn't gone more than a few yards when the glint of sunlight on bright metal caught my eye. Looking up I saw, high above us, a large black dog sitting upright and alert on a huge boulder which was embedded in the mountain slope. Around its neck it wore a broad leather collar, festooned with gleaming six-inch spikes. Beside the dog sat a tall muscular man. His broad grin made me realise that he had been watching us unobserved for a long time. I looked up at him and smiled back, conscious of my city-bred lack of awareness. His smile broadened and he nodded. I raised a hand in acknowledgement and walked on feeling elated and strangely secure, as if he was watching over us, keeping us safe. I was still buoyed up when we reached Rogi.

Rogi consisted of several farmhouses scattered across the side of the valley, and a very small school. Near the school was a flat, square piece of ground big enough for a bus to make a five-point turn; the end of the line for motorised transport. Outside one of the houses two middle-aged women sat. They were powerful, well-fed women, dressed in *Salwar Kameeze**, wearing Kullu caps over their oiled and plaited hair. One was teasing wool, and the other sat at a spinning wheel. They smiled.

'It's too hot to stand in the sun,' the older one said in Hindi. 'Come. You must be thirsty.'

---

* The *Salwar Kameeze* is a long shift worn over pajama-like trousers. Kulla caps are round, flat-topped headgear made of velvet material and normally bright green or red.

We sat down with them in the shade outside the door of her house and drank cool water. They brought us sun-dried apricots and pears, and were obviously pleased at our enjoyment of this special treat. We asked about buses and they told us we were in luck. The bus back to Kalpa 'would come before dark' — only a three-hour wait!

When it started to rain, we took cover inside the doorway. Sitting and talking of our respective lives, they laughed at my appalling Hindi. Warmth and friendliness were give freely and unselfconsciously. They showed us how to tease the wool to make it fit for spinning and how to spin it into yarn. Suman, our hostess and the older of the two, asked us questions about our lives in Delhi, while her young sister-in-law, Arti, explained to Sean how to spin the wool.

I told Suman about the dog with the spikes round his neck and she said that it was common for shepherds to equip their dogs with collars such as these to protect them from the snow leopards of which there were many in the area.* 'But,' she said, 'no shepherd would be there at this time of the year, for this is when the goats and sheep are taken to the higher pastures.' I described the man's powerful physique, and how I felt good simply by seeing him. 'You have seen Sangratan,' she said, smiling. 'No wonder you are in such a jolly mood.' I assured her it was their hospitality, but she and Arti both laughed. 'He has that power,' said Suman. 'All who see him feel the joy of living. He is *the* Amchi, a great healer of bodies and of souls. We are blessed that he has returned.'

---

* Since the leopards kill by attacking the throat of their prey, these collars were a highly-effective defence.

For the next hour or so the women regaled us with Sangratan's exploits. 'There is no Amchi to compare with him,' Suman said. They told tales of Sangratan's miraculous cures, of magical transformations of personalities, of his telephathic powers and ability to communicate with animals, and of his over-powering sex appeal. Arti even claimed that he was immortal. We sat and listened, bemused by their claims for this travelling healer.

Finally, as the evening drew in, we heard the distant rumbling of the bus. It was late. Outside the house people started to congregate, appearing out of the gloom. There were men with huge sacks of cereal, itinerant traders with large square packs which appeared to contain cloth, a farmer with a full-grown live sheep and shepherds with piles of sheepskins. All day we had seen no more than a handful of people, and now, suddenly, as if from nowhere, thirty or more people had appeared.

The ramshackle bus rumbled on to the square patch of land, and we offered our thanks and said goodbye to our new friends. We stood on the square and watched as, with much shouting and nervous laughter from the other prospective passengers, the bus manoeuvred backwards and forwards. A grim-faced driver, oblivious to the black humour of the more vocal elements of the crowd, at each manoeuvre took the bus perilously close to the sheer 2,000-feet drop at the edge of the tiny square. At last the bus was in position facing back down the track towards Kalpa, and it was safe for us to climb aboard.

We were the last to get on. Leathery hands helped us up over piles of sheepskins, sacks of grain, and the bundles of cloth which had been unceremoniously dumped in the doorway. The sheep was driven towards the back of the bus, and we took the remaining seats.

The bus was like most Indian buses: old, dilapidated, and in a state of disrepair which would have had it condemned as unroadworthy in most other countries. The back window had been replaced by a sheet of polythene, and the noise coming from the exhaust told us that it had no silencer. Most worrying, we had seen that all four tyres had no tread at all. Off we hurtled down the mountain track, careening over the rocks and boulders, spraying gravel into the abyss to our right. Quickly we reached the area near where Sangratan had been sighted. I looked up but could see neither man nor dog in the encircling gloom.

It began to rain again. The bus rushed on, bouncing in and out of the potholes, swerving around blind bends. We gripped the seats in front of us. The single working, misaligned headlight illuminated a small section of the road in front of us, enough for us to make out the edge of the narrow track and the beginning of the chasm. The three of us huddled together; three city-bred, ashen-faced passengers expecting the worst, silently praying.

The only other silent passenger was the sheep. It stood in the aisle at the back, serene and sure-footed as the bus bucked and bounced, swung and swerved, through the rain and the darkness, unaware of the fact that we were only inches from certain death. As for the other passengers, they were all busy chatting, making new friends, joking with old ones; smiling, laughing and sharing.

At last we reached the flatter farm land high above Kalpa. Soon we saw the farmhouse where we were staying and we called out to the driver to stop. The other passengers said goodbye as we alighted and thankfully set foot on solid ground, happily ignoring the rain in our relief to be home.

Back in the dry warmth of the farmhouse we changed our clothes and ate a simple meal of *dal* and *subzi* (pulses and vegetables). Sean was exhausted. As soon as he finished eating he crawled into bed and was asleep within minutes. I arranged his covers, kissed his brow, and stepped outside into the warm night air. The rain had stopped. I sat down on the rough veranda and gazed out across the valley.

Though the night was young, the almost full moon was already high in the sky. There were stars in abundance. A gentle breeze was blowing and the air was scented with wild thyme and pine. The moonlight accentuated the vastness of the landscape; the mountains seemed bigger, nearer, more powerful, more alive. Those dark brooding areas the moonlight did not illuminate seemed sad and lonely.

My wife sat down beside me and her hand found mine. We sat in silence, two small, transient creatures confronted by the age-old vastness of the stars, the sky and the mountains. On the far side of the valley someone had lit a fire, a flickering pinprick of light announcing another tiny human presence in the beautiful shadowy vastness.

Suddenly, for no apparent reason, my eyes welled with tears. I felt extremely sad and I did not understand why. I had no reason, as far as I could see, to be sad, or feel sorry for myself. I had all the accoutrements of a successful life: a well-paid job, a wonderful partner, a son of whom I was exceptionally proud, and the usual house, car and other material trappings of the successful professional. Sitting there in this beautiful magical land, holding the hand of the woman I loved, I realised that there was something missing in my life – and I didn't know what it was.

Later that night, I lay in bed unable to sleep. In my mind I ran through all of the reasons I had to be happy and I decided I had no right to feel sorry for myself. I thought of the hardships that the people of these mountains cheerfully faced; I thought of the warmth and kindness of Arti and Suman, women who freely offered us their hospitality, their company and their precious dried fruits; I thought of the friendly greetings of the men carrying their heavy loads uphill in the noon-day sun; and I thought of the passengers on the bus making new friends, sharing their joys with each other despite knowing that they were hurtling along inches away from oblivion. I marvelled at these people; at their joy in giving, without expectation of any kind of return; at their friendliness to strangers even as they struggled with the heaviest of burdens; and at their zest for life, even in the most perilous of circumstances.

I felt almost envious. Like most in the 'developed' world, I had more material goods and services than these people would ever have. I didn't have to face the deprivations that they had to face almost daily, and I could travel in relative safety wherever I liked. Compared to them, my life was full of luxury and privilege. Yet they seemed so full of the happiness of life compared to me and all the other people in my social circle. Why were they so fulfilled, so full of joy? What made them so hospitable despite their material shortages? What was their secret?

I pondered and dozed, my thoughts racing. I was too tired

either to think clearly or to stop thinking. Sangratan's smiling face flashed in front of my eyes, and I remembered Suman and Arti's stories which exalted his wisdom, perception and healing powers. I remembered how, though I had seen him only from a distance and no words were spoken between us, I had been filled with euphoria. I remembered Suman's calling him 'the healer of bodies and souls'. She had said that he made everyone feel good. Maybe he could clear my confusion, relieve my sadness. As sleep began to overtake me, I even started to wonder about the sheep in the bus – maybe it knew something I didn't.

I slept fitfully and was up and dressed a little before dawn. I gently woke a very sleepy Abha and told her that I was going to find Sangratan and that I would be back by lunchtime. 'Mmm hmm,' she mumbled with a sleepy smile, and snuggled down under the quilt. She was sound asleep when I walked out the door to begin my search.

2

• •

The Lessons
of Life

The farmers of the Himalayas rise before dawn. As soon as there is light men, women and children are outside tending to livestock or working in their fields. Daylight is precious and not one bit of it is wasted. As I followed the stream through the fields towards the place where I had seen Sangratan, they smiled and spoke in greeting. Sometimes the stream came within a few yards of their dwellings and, as I passed, the women would call out and invite me to eat with the family. There was friendliness everywhere. I politely refused, and contrasted their attitude with that of the property-owning people of my homeland. Somehow I could not imagine a warm greeting from an English landowner if a stranger walked past their doors at dawn.

My plan was to get back as soon as possible to where I had last seen Sangratan, so instead of following the track we had taken the day before I was following the course of the mountain stream which ran through the fields and pastures. This way was all downhill and much quicker. The stream crossed the track we had taken near the end of the pasture land, only a kilometre or so from the steep barren area where I had seen Sangratan. I had made good time and the sun had not yet cleared the high mountains on the far side of the valley when I reached the last farmhouse before the track.

In the small field outside the traditional, earth-roofed house, two men and two small children were repairing an irrigation channel. The elder child, a girl, was no more than six years old, and the boy no more than four. As I entered the field the two men looked up and the older man, who appeared to be about thirty, greeted me in a language I did not understand. The children smiled and waved shyly. I placed my hands together in the traditional Indian greeting and with a slight bow said, 'Namaste.' All of them copied my gesture. I walked on. As I was passing the house a voice called out to me in English.

'You are looking for me, Mr Bill?'

I turned sharply, surprised to hear my name. There, at the side of the house, knelt Sangratan, tying up his bedding roll. The dog, large, black and minus its fearsome collar, sat on its haunches beside him. Sangratan stood up and turned to face me. I was surprised at how tall he was. Most of the inhabitants of the area were no more than five feet eight and many were considerably smaller. Sangratan was a little over six feet tall. He was bare-headed and his silver-grey hair was swept back from his wide forehead. He stared at me with dark brown eyes, as if he was reading my thoughts. 'I can see you were looking for me.' He smiled.

My mind was racing. He had been facing away from me. How did he know I was there? How did he know my name? He seemed to have known I would come.

'Namaste ji. Were you expecting me?' I blurted out.

'Namaste. I thought you would come,' he said softly.

He motioned to a patch of cleared ground next to the stream and invited me to sit. A tall, pretty young woman came out of the house and Sangratan introduced her as Tulsi, the wife of the two men and the mother of the children I had just passed. He introduced himself. 'I am Sangratan and this,' he said, gesturing to the dog, 'is Kirti.' The dog stood up, and walked over to Sangratan.

It sat down next to him, head held high, proud and alert. Pleasantries were exchanged. *Chai* (tea) was offered and accepted, and Tulsi excused herself to prepare the drink.

There was a silence. Sangratan sat waiting for me to speak. I could not find the words I wanted and I didn't know where to start. After what seemed like an age, words started to come tumbling out. I told Sangratan that I had sought him so that I could learn why the people of this region seemed so happy and full of joy despite their material poverty, the harshness of the environment, the dangers they faced and the relative isolation of one family from the other. Sangratan's smile broadened. 'Are you sure that these are the questions you need the answer to?' he said.

I felt like a babbling idiot. Now I was sitting in front of him, I wasn't sure *what* I wanted to know. Sensing my discomfort, Sangratan decided to lessen my uneasiness. 'The people here are not isolated Bill-*ji*,' he said with warmth. 'They have each other. Unlike in your world, they are taught that everyone is a friend until he proves otherwise. They are not taught to "beware of strangers". For them there is no such thing as a "stranger", only a person who they do not know yet. They are taught that if you treat people you do not know with warmth and kindness, respect and generosity, you are much more likely to be treated well in return.' Sangratan paused, staring at my face. His eyes seemed to search deep inside me. I felt distinctly vulnerable.

After a moment or so it seemed as if he had finished his assessment of me and had decided to continue. 'This is one small part of the Lessons of Life that we all learn at our mother's knee.' A teasing look came to his face. 'I think even the children of your

Raj were taught this, but by the time they had come to this land they had forgotten it.' Even as he spoke I could see my mother in my mind's eye, hear the words she had repeated so many times: 'If you want people to be nice to you, you must be nice to them.' I looked up at him without answering. Again he seemed to be looking deep within me. Finally he said, 'I will tell you what you need to know.'

So it was that in the warmth of a Himalayan summer morning, beside a gushing stream as the sun rose over the snow-peaked mountains, Sangratan told me of the origins of the Lessons of Life. What follows are his words as I remember them.

All life is hard and, often, as outside influences and forces pull us this way and that, we bury deep inside us what we would really like, but we think we cannot have. In ancient times an approach to living was formulated so that all men and women could live life harmoniously together and pursue their personal wants and desires in the most effective way possible.

In the most ancient of times through trial and error, experience and reason, men and women learnt to live harmoniously together and with the world. But men and women are not perfect. They constantly change. They develop and grow, age and decline. They move on. They forget. They become distracted. Even with the best of intentions they sometimes stray from that which gives them joy. The great strength of human beings, their quest for improvement, often causes them to move away from what makes them fulfilled. They become narrow-sighted and obsessive.

Here in these mountains, many centuries ago, wise men realised that the problems which caused people to be unhappy were the result of the changes life brings, and people's inability to cope with their changed situations and perceptions. They decided to codify an approach to life which could be used to teach people how to live life to the full, and overcome the obstacles that nature presents.

Before the time of Buddha, the first Lessons of Life were written down. Learned men took this code for living to Tibet, China and other parts of India. In these ancient centres of learning and reason the original, codified Lessons of Life were supplemented, changed and expanded. Over the centuries new sections were added and older ones modified.

The final version of the Lessons of Life was written on scrolls shortly after the time of Buddha, by Tenzin, the greatest of the Amchi. Tenzin taught the Lessons of Life wherever he travelled and soon other Amchi and many monks and *lamas* also took up the teachings. Some of those who could write, wrote down what they had learnt, and so there came into being several versions of the Lessons of Life.

One day when travelling through the Rohtung, Tenzin disappeared, and neither he nor the original Lessons of Life were ever seen again. Over the centuries most of the other versions of the Lessons of Life have been destroyed, and all that remains are a few fragments kept as relics by monks or priests. Now the Lessons of Life are to be found, in a complete form, only in the heads of the true Amchi, for it is their duty to learn and memorise the lessons and pass them on to their successors.

It is also the duty of the true Amchi to teach the Lessons of Life, so that people are helped to live life to the full and maximise the joys life brings.

———◆———

As Sangratan explained the origins of the Lessons of Life, I found his deep voice and slight lisp strangely hypnotic. His eyes which had seemed watchful and probing, softened, and as I listened I found myself picturing an idyllic past. When he had stopped speaking I continued to imagine the wonderful world of Tenzin and the other Amchi, where men and women lived in harmony. Finally I looked up to see Tulsi had arrived with the *chai*. I had been lost in my imagining. They were both smiling indulgently at me. Sangratan shook his head. 'The world was never that good Bill-*ji*,' he said. 'If it had been, the Lessons of Life would not have been needed.'

3

The First Lesson of Life

The sun had risen high in the sky and we followed Kirti into the shade by the side of the house. We drank the hot sweet masala tea and Sangratan explained that the first Lesson of Life helps you find the answer to the questions: Who am I? What should I be doing?

These are the words of Sangratan:

———————◆———————

The First Lesson of Life you must learn is to determine what you value, and how much you value it. For if you are not clear what you value, you will never be fulfilled; you will waste your life and never find joy. The First Lesson of Life is, therefore, to keep in front of you what you value most. Then you can go on to decide what you want, and how much you want it in relation to the other things that life presents.

Life is about change. Everything changes. Even these mountains, solid and seemingly ageless, change. We change. At the beginning of our lives all of us obtain sets of values. We call some things 'good' and some things 'bad'. We value everything according to our needs, our understanding, what we have been told, what we sense and what we learn is right. We determine our values and our values determine us. Our values define us, as a group, and one from the other. But we change. We learn and forget, strive and succeed, or strive and fail. Often what we most value changes with time and circumstance. What seemed very important at a particular age, in one set of circumstances, may have hardly any importance to us when we are older, in different circumstances. A thirsty man sees great value in water and desires to have his fill. The same man when drowning curses it and wishes to be free from it.

People want different things at different times for life is for-ever moving. Some want to be happily married, to have children. Some want their wives to love them. Some want their husbands to show they care. They give high value to a soft word, for it is a rarity in their lives. Some want a large farm, a fine cow or lots of money. Some people do not know what they value and do not know what they want. They want things because they are there. They are like goats in a field of maize, eating and eating and never considering the effects on their stomachs until they are too bloated to move freely. People often appear to have everything, yet they suffer from feeling unfulfilled, confused, disgruntled or simply unhappy.

Sometimes our values change yet our behaviour, through habit or thoughtlessness, continues as before. This makes us increasingly frustrated and unhappy. Friendships are lost, relationships break down, we become estranged from our children, from our friends, from our family and our own true selves. We let circumstances dictate our actions and we take for granted our feelings, and the people and things we value most. Life presents so many different choices that we lose sight of, and do not pursue, that which is most important to us.

The Lessons of Life recognise that we cannot have it all. Everything has a value and everything has to be earned. We should pursue what we value most at the time we value it most.

Obtaining the things we truly value brings us joy.

The first question we must ask ourselves is: what is important? This is not easy. Many people get the answer wrong. We are told by others what we should value. Sometimes we suppress what we value because it conflicts with the values of those we hold dear. We grow up to put great value on many things, but we also have many things thrust upon us by others.

The First Lesson of Life teaches us that we need to answer these questions:

*   What do I really value?
*   Why do I value it/them/him/her?
*   What is most important to me?

When we give honest answers to these questions, we can give a clear purpose to our lives.

Be warned! The answers to these questions change from person to person, from time to time, from situation to situation. Most of us value our families and friends. We also give high value to good health, to our religion, to our beliefs, to the activities that give us pleasure. There are so many things we give great value to, for many different reasons, but everything changes. Sometimes the change in our values is dramatically quick, sometimes so very slow that it is not until we 'stop to think' that we realise a change has occurred.

Consider. We give great value to our mothers, and for many different reasons. They gave us life. They sustained us when we could not look after ourselves. They clothed us, fed us, nursed us and protected us. They taught us, advised us and cared for us and kept us company. For all these things we give them great value. However, as we grow older we look after ourselves. We learn from others. We have partners to care for us and keep us company. Sometimes we reject what our parents have taught us. Sometimes we find more pleasure in the closeness of our new companions. As our mothers' strength declines, they need our care, and for *us* to protect *them*. As our relationship with them changes, why we value them also changes. We value them not so much for what they give us, for their powers to give wane; increasingly we value them for what they have given us in the past. But the past is not before our eyes as the present is. Unless we make an effort we cannot see the past as clearly as we should. The Lessons of Life teach us to make that effort.

We all value our mothers but many do not see clearly why. We speak of their efforts for us but we gradually lose sight of them. By regularly asking ourselves why we value some thing or some person, we help ourselves to appreciate the object or person we value better, and understand ourselves more. This is true not only of objects and people but of principles, relationships and desires as well.

The third question we ask ourselves – What is most important to me? – is to determine if there is conflict between what we value most and what we think is most important for us. To live in harmony with ourselves there must be harmony between what we think is most important and what we most value. So often when we see those who are unhappy we find that what they value most has been lost within them, and overcome by things they do not really care about. By regularly thinking about what we value, we ensure that we always pursue what is most important to us.

To determine what is most important to us, we must ask ourselves these further questions:

* What do I spend most of my time wishing for?
* What is it that I have always wanted?
* What is it that gives me most pleasure?
* What do I most regret?
* What ways of behaving do I find most admirable in others and myself?

Is there a contradiction between our values, and what we spend most of our lives wishing, craving, wanting or working for? If there seems to be a contradiction between what we spend most of our time working for or desiring, and our most important values, we must reassess what we believe to ensure our values reflect the true importance we give objects, creatures or people. Remember, it is necessary to do this because so often in life, lesser values can overwhelm our most important ones, and we can lose track of what we really cherish.

For those of us who want to be in control of our lives, this process of value assessment is the very first step, for it is these values by which we give purpose to our lives. However, this assessment should not be seen as a once-in-a-lifetime event.

The first Lesson of Life is to see the value in everything and to always know at any one time what we value most so that we can give that most importance. To do this we must continuously reassess our relationships with objects and all sentient creatures.

Sangratan finished his discourse on the First Lesson of Life and began to stand up. Tulsi quickly moved to help him.

'Hard ground, old, cold bones,' said Sangratan in Hindi, as he placed a gentle, steadying hand on her shoulder. He then said something to her in a language I did not understand and she smiled, displaying beautiful white teeth. 'She greatly values helping others,' Sangratan said, his muscular arm on her shoulder in a display of genuine affection. 'And she is greatly valued for it,' he said, with a chuckle. I turned to see her husbands Vivek and Vikram, and her children looking proudly at her. It was obvious that friendship, kindness and selflessness were greatly valued here.

Tulsi brought drinking water from the stream. Unfiltered and untreated, it was clean and pure. Almonds, too, fresh from the tree with a taste and texture unlike anything I had experienced before. We sat and drank, and ate and talked, and the day became hotter.

Sangratan found pleasure in everything around him, and his pleasure was infectious. For him everything was a wonder, everything was a joy: a passing butterfly, the scent of pine on the smallest of breezes, the breeze itself, a bird, a flower, the scurrying of ants and other small insects. In everything he found a reason to be happy. The children scrambled into his arms and he enjoyed their nearness. 'There is so much to value Bill-*ji*,' he said. 'Happiness comes from everything of value.'

The morning passed, a truly sensual morning. Sangratan's words had inspired me to look at everything with new eyes and to ask, 'Do I value this?' I marvelled at the light of the day, the joy of seeing, of touching, smelling and sensing, at the warmth of the sun, at the wonder of the myriad life-forms busily pursuing their diverse activities, at the company of kind, giving people, the beauty of small children, and of young adults, and the dignity of the not-so-young. I found new happiness in so many things that only a few hours before I had taken for granted or not even noticed.

The sun was so high in the sky that the shadow beside the house had shrunk to a thin strip. We sat and talked while others worked nearby. Tulsi busied herself preparing *aloo* (potato) and beans, the men repaired tools. The children, who had listened patiently while Sangratan explained the First Lesson of Life, had gone back to the field where they were deepening the irrigation channel with their tiny hands. Sangratan sat repairing a tunic. Only Kirti and I were idle. She lay at Sangratan's feet, almost asleep.

Suddenly Kirti sat up, sniffing the breeze. Sangratan put down the tunic. Man and dog looked at each other.

'We have to go,' he said, and rose quickly to his feet.

Gathering his belongings, he apologised for his hasty departure. Goodbyes were said, and on ascertaining he was making his way towards the track which led back to where I was staying, I decided to walk with him. Promising Tulsi and her family we would meet again soon, we said our goodbyes and set off down the mountain following the stream.

We soon reached the track and turned left towards the farmhouse where my family and I were staying. After a hundred yards or so, Sangratan stopped.

'We go this way Bill-*ji*,' he said, pointing to a barely discernible trail winding down the steep slope towards the valley floor. 'We must leave you now, but we will meet again.'

I said my goodbyes, and man and animal quickly descended from view.

Walking back along the track to my wife and family, I wondered what had made Sangratan leave so abruptly, and I hoped that we would meet again soon, for I was eager to learn more of the Lessons of Life.

As I climbed the steep track that led to the farmhouse, I saw my wife waiting on the veranda. As she saw me her face lit up in greeting. That smile is something I value highly I thought to myself and, as the thought entered my head, I realised that it was one of the things I had begun to take for granted. I also realised it gave me pleasure not only when she smiled at me, but when she smiled at anything. I walked up to her, took her face in my hands and gazed at her.

'What?' she said, her smile turning quizzical.

'I greatly value your smiling face,' I said.

'Really?' she said, bemused. 'Is everything all right?'

'Never better,' I said, silently resolving to do my best to ensure she smiled more in future.

Sean had gone to Kalpa with some children from one of the nearby farms and we had the afternoon to ourselves. We sat and talked and I told her of my meeting with Sangratan, and what had transpired. I pointed out to her some of the joys that he had shown me. It seemed I was rediscovering how much I loved my wife and, in the process, I was beginning to discover a new me. I was starting to learn the Lessons of Life. By the evening we were both smiling almost constantly.

• •

4

The Second Lesson of Life

D ays passed. Happy days. We basked in the serenity of the mountains, the freshness of the air, the heady fragrance of wild thyme and the scents of the pine forest. We enjoyed warm sunny days and clear crisp nights. No wonder the gods had made these mountains their home. By day we walked, surrounded by majesty and beauty, among spectacular mountains and waterfalls, forests and snow-covered heights and, nestling within, small human habitats. Nature and man were at one. But there was no sign of Sangratan. We searched for him but he had simply disappeared.

On the fourth night after my meeting with him, I sat alone on the veranda, gazing up at the moonlit peaks. The night was young but the other two had gone to bed, exhausted after a day of walking the forest paths. I wondered what had become of Sangratan. The peaks of the Kinnuer Kailash were covered with a fresh fall of snow and a strong breeze had cleared the bright moonlit sky of clouds.

Suddenly, a fire flared in the pasture far to my right. It seemed to leap fully formed into existence, blazing brightly in the Himalayan night. Somehow I knew it must be Sangratan. I looked into the bedroom where Sean lay sleeping peacefully. Abha was still awake, reading. She looked up.

'I'm going out for a while,' I said. 'Don't wait up.'

'What?' she said.

'Sangratan's down in the pasture,' I said, in hope and expectation. 'I'll just nip over and see him.'

She gave me her slightly exasperated look. 'Can't it wait till morning?'

'I'll see you later,' I said. 'Sweet dreams.'

I closed the bedroom door and, picking up a torch, walked out into the cool night air.

From the veranda the fire did not seem to be very far away. I judged it was no more than a half-kilometre or so. Distance is difficult to judge in the dark but I felt I had my bearings. Before setting out, I peered into the moonlight and was certain that the campfire was in a pasture above one of the apple orchards which line the lower valley slopes. I calculated that it would take me twenty minutes to reach it.

Half an hour later I was still walking and stumbling, and the campfire was still a distant beacon. Doubt had set in. I began to imagine arriving at the fire only to find it belonged to a shepherd or a traveller. I looked back the way I had come. The mountain side was in shadow, and the lights from the farmhouse had disappeared. Every so often a dog would challenge my journey, barking ferociously as I stumbled over yet another unseen obstacle. Soon dogs were barking throughout the valley. I began to feel lost and very foolish, as well as apprehensive that a fierce dog would come hurtling out of the darkness.

Finally, the farmhouses were left behind and, after more stumbling, the campsite came into view. As I drew nearer I could make out the shadowy figure of a man seated with his back to me. I peered through the darkness searching the area the fire illuminated. Where was Kirti? Definitely not near the fire. I was torn between thinking that this had been a wild goose chase or, worse, that at any moment I would be the victim of an over-zealous guard dog.

I approached the campfire cautiously. Sangratan turned and smiled. 'It is you Bill-*ji*. Welcome,' he said.

'*Namaste-ji*,' I said. 'Where is Kirti?'

He waved his hand towards the shadows. 'Resting,' he said. 'As we all should be.'

My face fell. I had not considered the time, or his need for sleep and solitude. I had stumbled all this way not thinking at all about whether my visit would be appropriate.

'But you have come such a long way in the dark, Bill-*ji*. Your need must be great,' Sangratan said in a kindly tone.

'That is because I greatly value your wisdom,' I said.

Sangratan chuckled. '*Acha*! The *baacha** of the Raj has learnt to speak with a honeyed tongue.'

He beckoned to me to sit beside him and I did so, accepting the water that he offered. It felt good to be in his presence for he seemed always to be full of joy. 'So how are you?' he said with a soft chuckle.

'I am well, Sangratan. These last few days I have begun to realise all that I value, and there is so much. From the smallest of creatures scurrying to provide for its young, to the trees and plants, to my wife's smile. Once I started looking, I found value everywhere.'

'And where do you find the things you value most?' asked Sangratan, smiling even more broadly.

---

*'I see! The child of the Raj . . .'

'I find new value in so many things,' I said. 'In the flight of birds, in the scenery, in the people I meet, but most of all my family. Those that care for me, and in whose company I find stimulation.'

'It is a strange word, this "stimulation",' he said quizzically, 'but you are learning well. It is right that you find great value in the presence of living things, strangers and those you know, for they all go to shape your life and make it what it is. And it is good that you find the greatest value in your family, those closest to you, who sustain and nurture you most. The people of this valley know that men and women need to live in harmony with each other and a multitude of living things; helping and nurturing each other for their mutual benefit. They also know that all things of value are shaped by living things. The smallest and largest of living things contribute to this land's shape and form and when we can see the value they give, we give them their true value. The closer we can live in harmony with a multitude of life-forms, the more we prosper, man, beast and plants. Where beasts and plants, insects and birds do not survive, neither does man.'

Sangratan fell silent, a slight frown on his broad features. He was looking at me but I realised he was contemplating something else.

I considered his words. I remembered watching the insects moving leaves and minute quantities of material, shaping the world in their own tiny way. It began to be clear to me how the actions of the smallest living things contribute to the broader picture and I thought of the pleasure I had derived from sitting in the pasture that afternoon, a pasture shaped and developed by millions of single seeds of grass, and the ages-old industry of microscopic life-forms and tiny animals. I contemplated the smallness of the human settlements in this vast land as well as the millions of human actions, large and small, over tens of thousands of years, along with the actions of uncountable millions of other life-forms, that have created, shaped, re-created and reshaped the physical world. I was lost in my thoughts. When I finally looked up it was to see Sangratan smiling broadly, his face seeming to glow in the light of the blazing fire. We sat in silence for a considerable time, contemplating small things, small actions.

Finally, my meditation over, and at what I thought was the right moment, I broke the silence.

'But all this raises a question, Sangratan-*ji*,' I said. 'There is so much to value but I don't know where to start pursuing what I value. What should I be doing?'

He smiled at me, the broad smile that came so quickly to him, his eyes luminous in the firelight.

'Before you start to pursue what you value,' he said, 'you must understand the need to appreciate the power and value of small things. By your small actions you shape your large actions, as all large creatures and objects are shaped and determined by smaller objects and creatures.' He paused. 'I can see you are beginning to realise this, so I will tell you the Second Lesson of Life. But first you must tell me how you came here tonight.'

I told him everything; about seeing the fire, taking the torch and walking through the dark. I told him how the dogs had barked, and about my fear of being attacked; about how I had misjudged the location and distance, and my apprehension when I finally arrived. Sangratan listened patiently, nodding and smiling encouragement as I explained. When I had finished, he said quietly: 'It was good that you could always see the fire, which marked where you wanted to get to, otherwise you could still be stumbling about in the dark. You see, Bill-*ji*, we always get to our destination the better when we can see where we want to be. Of course, the clearer we can see the path, the easier the journey. However, if we cannot see or do not know where our destination is, we are very likely to get lost. The Second Lesson of Life helps us along the difficult path to where we want to be.'

A gust of wind caused the fire to flare and sparks to cascade. Sangratan paused. Taking a piece of wood from a pile beside him he placed it on the fire. More sparks. He pulled the rough blanket over his head and tighter around his body, and proceeded to tell me the Second Lesson of Life.

This is what Sangratan said:

O nce we have learnt to keep before us what we value most, we must learn how to walk the path to personal fulfilment. The Second Lesson of Life will help us do this, for it shows us how to plan our journey so that we can maximise the joys that life can bring. Whereas the First Lesson teaches that we must constantly meditate on what we value, the Second Lesson shows us how to pursue that which we value most so that we can nurture and develop it and strive to seek greater joy.

The Second Lesson reminds us that in this ever-changing world we always need to think ahead so that we can sustain that which we value, and develop that which we long for. We know that in spring we must work towards the crops of autumn. In summer we must make provision to see us through the snows of winter. All men and women know this, they know they will not prosper long if they do not. However, sometimes, even when concerned with what they value, they fail to understand that permanence is an illusion. The cycles of living things affect us all. The fields of summer provide us with an abundance, but by the time spring comes, almost all the harvest has disappeared. So it is with all that we value. We must constantly strengthen and renew that which we value highly and seek a path to that which we value and have not yet obtained.

The Second Lesson of Life also reminds us that we cannot have everything at once and that we must keep a balance between what we have that we value, and any new objects or relationships of value we wish to pursue. Wise people have always known this. Each year we harvest our crops. At the appropriate times we sow, cultivate and reap. We feast, preserve and store. Always our vision is fixed on the present and on the future at the same time. Always we are informed by the past. Each day we work towards preserving and using what is, and each day we work towards producing for the future. Each new day we change our environment and in the process we change our lives. We preserve and store and maintain last year's crop while irrigating, planting and cultivating for the harvest which is to come. So it is with our children; we nurture and care for them today, so that they will become what we want them to become tomorrow. So it should be with all the things we value, with our wives or husbands, with our friends, and all living things. We preserve and maintain our relationships today, while working to strengthen and develop them for tomorrow.

Whereas the First Lesson of Life teaches us to keep before us what we value most, the Second Lesson of Life teaches us that each day we are building tomorrow. It tells us to work towards tomorrow so that we nurture the changes that come to the things we value. To do this we must keep in front of us what we want the future to bring. Without care and cultivation and nurturing, the fields are over-run with inedible plants and our crops fail. Without care and cultivation and nurture, all the things we value fall into disarray. We plant our seeds so that we can thrive and prosper on the harvest. Each day we tend them so that they are as fine and healthy as we can make them. We fertilise and irrigate, weed and replant and do any number of tasks to ensure that the harvest is as good as it can be. So it should be with everything we value. The Second Lesson of Life teaches us that to turn our dreams into reality we have to care and nurture them as we do our crops, and it reminds us that this is an everyday activity – not a once-in-a-while activity.

Every day the good farmer seeks what is best for his plants. Every day he attends to his crops, sowing or planting, weeding or irrigating, harvesting or preserving. So it is with all things. The husband who, every day, attends to his wife's needs, will see her and their relationship grow and prosper. The traveller who walks every day towards his destination will get there much quicker than the one who wanders aimlessly, or the one who does not walk at all, or the one who does not concentrate on where he wants to go.

The First Lesson of Life helps us see our possible destinations and the Second reminds us that everything has its time. Wise men and women understand this and know when to give importance to what they value, when to plan, when to act and when to move on. As the wise farmer understands the seasons and what needs to be done and when, so does the wise man or woman. Only the ignorant expect the crops to grow without being planted and nurtured, or the flowers to bloom without watering. The nurturing of whatever we value requires effort and patience on our part but once we are sure of what we value we quickly see what has to be done. People who cannot live in harmony with those they value should look to the efforts they are making. Is theirs the right kind of nurturing, are they expecting the relationship to be the same in the cold of winter as it was in spring or the harvest time? Better to work towards the new spring, when they can replant and renew.

The people of these mountains know that calamity and disaster come easily. Crops fail, avalanches are common. The harshness of the winters takes its toll. Living in harmony is not easy. They know how swiftly they can lose that which they value, if they do not keep their eyes on the future and work to develop it. They know that they must look to the future in the same way as the wise traveller keeps his destination in his mind's eye.

Those who have learnt the Second Lesson of Life meditate in the morning and reflect in the evening. Each morning they consider what it is they seek to preserve, and what it is they seek to develop. When they do this they hold in front of themselves a vision of what they wish to develop and a time when that vision will be made manifest. In the evening they reflect on what they have done during that day to preserve, develop and nurture what they value. During the day they are conscious that they must share their concerns and plans with those to whom they are closest.*

———————

Sangratan finished speaking. For a brief moment he wore a look of profound sadness. He stared hard into the fire. When he looked up the broad smile was back but I realised how very disconcerting it was to see him when he was not smiling.

'So Bill-*ji*,' he said. 'Are you now ready to develop and nurture what you value?'

'I think so,' I said, 'but if you will give a little shove to get me started I would greatly appreciate it.'

Sangratan let out a deep throaty chuckle. 'What is this "shove"?' He laughed. 'How is this for a "shove"? Each morning you ask yourself how you can nurture that which is important to you. Think of some small action which will develop each of the main things you value, pledge to yourself to do these small acts before the evening comes and the day is gone. Do not pledge to do too many, nor to do acts which require extraordinary effort. A few very small acts (not more than six) is quite sufficient. At the end of the day meditate on what you have done, count off your efforts to develop what you value, and look forward to the new day coming

---

* Sangratan said later that it was not necessary to meditate and reflect every single day, but regularly and often.

as a new opportunity. In this way, every day you will enhance what you value and bring joy to yourself. And while you do this, remember that great events, acts, states of being, are simply the culmination of millions of small events and acts.'

'But what values should I develop?' I said.

Sangratan took a branch from the pile of wood and poked the fire. More sparks. Flames leapt from the embers. He stared into the fire. Another long silence. Finally he looked up. I knew I had disappointed him but did not as yet understand why.

'You see, Bill-*ji*,' he said, in his soft kindly tone, 'you first need to meditate on the values of life you understand yourself, and to discover what it is that is most important to you, and only then decide how you wish to develop that which you value. The sadness of life in towns and cities is that people do not meditate on what they value, but are overwhelmed by the values espoused by others. In this valley they have a saying: "Get a television, lose your children." In the towns there are so many new influences on you, enjoining you to value all sorts of things: this TV machine, schools, those by whom you are employed, the newspapers. You become like a bucket overflowing with the values others want of you. Value this or that item, or this way of doing things, or this way of thinking. What *you* truly value is often buried. Meditating on what you truly cherish will lead you to who you really are, and once you know yourself you will know where you want to be in the future. Knowing what you value and how much you value it, is the fire that illuminates the dark. The world now is full of so many lights that others want you to walk towards. Meditating helps keep your eyes firmly fixed on the light of what you value. It is a way of keeping that light in front of you so that you can walk towards that light, one day at a time, one step at a time . . .'

His voice trailed off. He was gazing out into the dark, a soft smile of contentment on his face. He turned to me and with genuine affection said, 'Ask yourself these questions: How can I enhance and develop that which I value? How can I fill my life with that which I value most? What can I do today to move towards this new state? At the end of the day ask these questions: What have I done today to enhance what I value? What have I done to develop what I value? These are questions you should meditate on. The answers are within you, Bill-*ji*, as they are within all of us.'

His words had a strange effect on me. I knew that he was right. I knew that if I did a he suggested I would find happiness, peace and harmony. I looked into his face and was reassured. His kindly eyes sparkled with happiness and contentment. The sadness of a few minutes ago had passed. He emanated kindness and caring and I felt safe sitting there swathed in his concern and affection. It was a strange feeling for a professional man in middle life suddenly to experience.

'Time for sleep, Bill-*ji*,' he said. Twisting the blanket into a different configuration he lay down on the hard ground beside the blazing fire. I peered out into the darkness, pulled my jacket around me, crept close to the fire and lay down to wait for the dawn light to find my way back to my wife and family.

I had a sleepless night on the hard ground, feeling guilty about staying out and worrying about wild animals. I searched the dark for Kirti, but could not see her. Sangratan slept, his soft snoring proclaiming blissful sleep. I waited the long hours for the dawn.

There must be some law which states that when you have not slept all night, with the dawn comes the moment when you drop off to sleep. So it was that, just as I was sinking into the most beautiful of slumbers, Sangratan's soft voice reached my ears.

'Dawn is breaking, Bill-*ji*. You must go.'

I opened my weary eyes. The fire was almost out, the darkness not quite as intense. This was dawn? I sat up. Grudgingly I accepted that Sangratan was right. The sun hadn't risen, but it was getting lighter. I could make out the shape of Kirti lying a little way from the campfire, awake and watchful in the fledgling dawn.

'Your family will be expecting you soon,' said Sangratan, looking warm and snug in a thick shawl made soft by years of use.

My wife will be going wild with concern, I thought, and struggled to my feet. 'You're right. I have to go. Abha will be frantic.'

'*Namaskar*,' said Sangratan, sitting up. 'We shall meet again soon.'

I said my goodbyes and left before he had got to his feet. Striding through the early morning gloom, I went down the mountain side as fast as the light would allow. By the time I reached the farmhouse it was light. The sun still had to force itself above the mountains, but dawn had definitely broken. I knocked gently on the farmhouse door and after a few seconds a very sleep Abha opened it. I put my arms around her. Her body was warm and soft from sleep. I held her close.

'I'm sorry,' I said. 'You must have been sick with worry.'

She snuggled closer. 'No,' she said. 'The old man delivered your message.'

'What message?' I asked. 'I had sent no message.'

She told me that an old man had turned up at the door only minutes after I had left the house. He told her that I would be out till dawn and not to worry. Who was he? The man she described bore a remarkable resemblance to Sangratan. It seemed to me that somehow he had managed to be at the campfire and at the farmhouse at the same time.

5

● ●

The Power of Meditation

I crawled into bed. The morning was still young, and I needed to rest. The bed felt wonderfully soft after the hard ground, and my sleep was deep and peaceful.

I awoke after a couple of hours, refreshed and eager to enjoy the day. The farmhouse had a 'bathroom' for visitors: a stone outhouse with a drainage hole in the floor and a corrugated tin roof. The bucket to hold the water was fed by a tap, the tap was fed by a plastic tank on the roof, and the tank was fed by a pipe from a stream that flowed through the field at the back of the house. The water was very, very cold. I bathed as quickly as possible, dipping my hand in the bucket and splashing a few drops of water on my sleep-warmed skin, then a soapy water smear and more splashes. I shivered my way through my toilet, seriously considering adopting the bathing habits of the locals who, traditionally, bathed once or twice a year.

My late breakfast consisted of parathas and pickles, and hot sweet tea — ideal fuel for a hard day's toil in the fields, but heart attack fodder for a middle-aged, overweight, deskwallah. It was delicious. I ate far more than my energy needs required, and then I meditated.

Never having done it before, I concentrated hard on what it was I valued, and then I asked the questions that Sangratan gave me. The answers that came from within suggested other questions I should ask myself. Why did I value it? Why this, not that? Then I asked myself what it was I wanted to change. What was it I wanted to get better? And then the 'when' questions. By when did

I want the new state of affairs to be in place? When should I start to make changes?

It was a clumsy attempt at meditation. I went round in circles. It was nothing like the transcendental meditation described to me by a friend in the flower-power 1960s. It was not the stream-of-consciousness meditation that comes from changing. This meditation was simply me putting time aside to concentrate and ponder on the things I valued; setting aside the time to ask myself the questions I had sometimes casually asked myself in the past, but had never followed up. This meditation was a conscious attempt to confront my values and search for ways to develop my life in accord with them. I held the thought of the good farmer in my mind. It was my attempt at the practical meditation of a practical person. It was a very clumsy attempt, but it worked.

I had given myself fifteen uninterrupted minutes to meditate and at the end of that time I had a lot of confusion, but I had made one major decision, and it did alter my life for the better. It was fifteen minutes well spent. It was easy to decide what it was that I valued most, for we all of us know what gives us the greatest joy (even if often we deny it). For me it was my son. What it was about him I valued most was a little more difficult to answer, for there were so many things. I set about trying to list the happiness Sean gave me, but some things were so obvious, and some were intangible. I cut short the list for, as I thought of him, it came to me that what I valued most was his company. It was foolishness on my part, but in listing the little things – his smile, his exuberance, his happiness, his wide-eyed innocence – I had begun to get bogged down in details. For all sorts of reasons, many to do with his virtues, some to do with my deeper psychological needs, I simply loved his company. I was aware of wanting to relive my relationship with my father, to give Sean the happiness my father gave me, so that I could understand better the happiness my father had got from our relationship, and in that way feel closer to my father once again.

I thought about what Sangratan had said about the little things in life and realised that all of Sean's little attributes made up the sum of him as it does with us all. I thought about what Sangratan had said about changes, and about how we change and how each day we bring a slightly different version of ourselves to the world, one changed by the experiences of the previous day. Then I thought about how Sean would grow up and leave as I grew up and left home. I thought about how my relationship with my father changed as he grew older and sick and frail, and I grew taller, stronger, more independent. I wept.

After I had wept, I knew with a certainty what I would do. I knew it rationally and emotionally. I would give Sean what my father had given me. I would enjoy Sean's company in the way that my father must have enjoyed mine those long years ago when I was a child, before life changed us and I went away. From the jumble of thoughts and half thoughts, of questions and half answers it had become obvious what to do. I would take a lunch break every day!

When I was a boy my school was only a few hundred yards from my home so I did not stay at school for lunch. My father worked in a factory making bus seats, and he had a compulsory hour for lunch. It took twelve minutes of brisk walking for him to get to our house from the factory, and twelve minutes to walk back.

He had timed it so that he did not waste a precious minute inside the factory that he hated so much. Thirty-six minutes for lunch at home where we would eat and talk. With a working week of five days that was three hours a week. One hundred and fifty hours a year for all of my childhood: 2,700 hours between birth and the age of eighteen. And such pleasant memories of talking and sharing, of having someone interested in me, and my day, each and every day.

So the result of my first meditation was to decide to take a lunch break when Sean got home from school. Since he arrives home at 2.30, it is a very late lunch break, but at that time we sit and snack and he tells me of his day, and I tell him about mine. We sit as my father and I sat in that time long ago, in the days when many fathers and sons sat and talked, as they sat and talked for generations before careers were invented. I thought of the other farmers in this valley; families working together, eating together, sharing each and every hardship, talking to each other all day long, toiling in common enterprise, living in harmony. Sangratan was right: for those who nurture such simple things great joy is found.

I finished my meditation and I told Abha of my decision that from now on I would have a lunch break to be there for Sean.

'Two innovations in your life,' she said. 'Your setting aside time to meditate, *and* planning to set aside more time for Sean. Good!' I smiled weakly as she continued. 'I must meet this Sangratan. He must be very special to keep you out all night, *and* cause you to meditate, let alone resolve to change your way of life!'

'It seems to me that you might have,' I said. 'As I told you, the man you described coming to the door last night could well have been him!'

'I thought you were supposed to be the sceptic in this relationship,' she said, seeming highly amused. 'Come on, then, let us go and see this great sage of yours.'

So we did. Arrangements were made. Sean went off on the long walk to Kalpa with some older boys from the neighbouring farms to see a cricket match. The village team were playing and the school had closed for the day so that the whole village could turn out to watch the match. The boys would follow the stream down the hill, cutting through the winding road which once was the ancient silk route from India to Tibet, while Abha and I took off through the almond and apple orchards heading for Sangratan's campsite of the night before.

It was a delightful walk. Beautiful butterflies flitted through the trees, skimming the marijuana plants which grew in wild profusion around the orchard's edge. The sun was high, and the sky a deep blue. A cool breeze tempered the heat, and the gurgling streams and myriad birdsong added to the immense charm of the experience. How different things are in the light of day, I thought, as I remembered my stumbling fearful journey of the previous night. I took Abha's hand and kissed her cheek. Better still the journey with some one you love I thought.

'What?' she said.

'The kiss was the message,' I said.

We walked on. Our route did not take us close to any farmhouses but along narrow pathways which delineated where one field ended and another began. No one made physical barriers here between farms, between people. Where walls existed they had been built to keep animals in (or out). I thought of Delhi and its walls and fences, but quickly, consciously, moved my mind back to the present, to this idyllic late morning paradise.

We followed our ears to a tumbling stream, drank our fill and, finding a comfortable spot under a tall tree, we sat and rested, enjoying the moment. In silence we sat side by side with out backs to the tree, delighting in the cool breeze, the smell of wild thyme and the butterflies. Rested and cooled, we got up without speaking, and strolled on. The bright sunlight and the clear sky gave every-thing a vividness that it had not had first thing that morning. I realised again what Sangratan meant when he said everything changes all the time!

In hardly any time at all we were at the site of Sangratan's camp, but there was no sign of him: no human debris, no flattened grass, no ash or blackened area, no sign of a fire. There was nothing to suggest any human had been there at all. I looked at the spot where I had lain: lush grass looking far softer than my sleepless night could testify to. It was not crushed or flattened, but swaying gently in the cool breeze. Where the fire had been, there was only soft soil and virgin rock.

I stood and stared around me. I looked back the way we had come. It was the way I had travelled early in the morning. This *was* the spot where Sangratan had built his camp with its huge fire, but there was no trace of it or of him.

'Well?' said Abha, in her I'm-not-amused tone. 'Where is he?'

'I swear he was here,' I said feebly, 'but it seems he's disappeared.'

'Without trace?' said Abha, an incredulous expression on her face. 'Perhaps you've got the wrong place,' she said with more than a hint of exasperation.

I knew I hadn't. This was the place. I recognised so many things in the immediate vicinity. I had lain in this spot and watched the dawn break. I had walked down this hillside on my way back to the farm only a few hours ago. This was the spot. Now it was as if he and I had never been there.

6

....

The Third Lesson
of Life

Days passed with no sign of Sangratan. The weather changed and it rained each day, a hard cold rain. We'd wake each morning to an overcast sky and the promise of more rain. The Kinnuer Kailash was transformed. On the high ground heavy snowfalls covered the whole range, seeming to change the very shape of the mountains. The sinister clouds blotted out the sun and the daytime temperature, which had been around 30 degrees Celsius, plummeted to single figures. The breeze turned into an icy wind, and at night the wind-chill factor brought temperatures very close to zero. We slept fully clothed, thankful for the heavy blankets.

For four days the atrocious weather continued. Four long days of standing at the window and watching the rain, of quick huddled walks bundled up in layers of T-shirts and sweat shirts and jumpers, cursing that we had not brought heavy coats. Four days of watching the clouds swirl around the mountain tops. At times thunder reverberated along the valley, rumbling and grumbling and finally bursting forth in loud roars. The streams became torrents, churning and spitting, battering those rocks foolish enough to stand in their way. Everywhere water was on the move, dripping off the roof, running down the paths, forming new streamlets which quickly found their way to the existing water courses. All this under a dark and brooding sky. It was easy to imagine that the gods were angry.

I was broody, too. Frustrated with the weather, with the disappearance of Sangratan, and with my attempts at meditation and reflection. I was also bothered by a recurring dream: I am alone in a house made of pine, a gigantic furnished holiday lodge with endless corridors and no exit. In my dream I wander the corridors looking in the rooms, looking out of the windows at a deserted seaside resort. I look in every room for Sangratan but when I finally find him he is sitting in the lotus position, his customary smile replaced by a scowl of displeasure. The dream always ends the same way: I am about to speak to him when I wake up . . .

My morning meditations on those rainy days were a shambles and I began seriously to reconsider the worth of the whole process. I found it very difficult to think clearly about the things I valued, and found my mind wandering or locked in conflict over what I valued more, this or that, them or it. It was not until the morning of the fourth day that I awoke to an understanding of what I was doing wrong.

On the third night the dream had returned: after much wandering down the endless corridors, this time I find the room where Sangratan is sitting in his usual lotus position. His face is expressionless. The scowl has disappeared and he sits with his eyes closed. I am about to say his name when his eyes open and he smiles at me. Before I could speak I woke up! It was morning and I somehow *knew* that when meditating I had to meditate on *one* value, or *one* object of value at a time.

I knew all sorts of new things! I *knew* that all value is relative, that all value is subjective in the sense that we shape the nuances of the values we are given, even when they are shared values, even when they seem objective. The great religions of the world all stress the illusory nature of existence. Almost all religious meditations seek to transcend the illusory nature and to know 'God', but I suddenly *knew* that was a separate process from what I was supposed to be attempting. I awoke knowing that, by examining my values, I was seeking to understand my inner self and my relationship with an ever-changing world. In examining each value I would redefine myself and the world. No wonder I was confused. I resolved to examine only one value per day.

Later in the day the rain stopped, the blue sky returned and on our side of the valley the air was heavy and still. In the distance the mountain tops were covered with heavy grey clouds from which the thunder continued to rumble. It seemed as if the gods were still not pleased, but had shifted their displeasure from us and were grumbling among themselves, shrouded in their clouds on their distant mountain tops.

We ventured out. We intended to take a long walk following the stream up towards the village of Pangi, but the ground was too wet and our path too steep and muddy. We returned to the farmhouse, thankful for the change in the weather, waiting for the land to dry out.

Days passed. The heat returned, the damp ground enhancing the fragrances and giving the evenings a romantic smokiness. We took our long walks, exploring new paths, going further into the less inhabited areas, ever hopeful of sighting Sangratan, but without success.

By the ninth day after my night-time meeting with Sangratan there was still no sight of him and I decided that he had moved on, and that I would probably not see him again. I imagined him striding out along one of the mountain passes, and calculated that even walking at a relatively comfortable pace he could have easily covered the eighty or so kilometres to the border, and be deep into Tibet by now.

On that ninth day Abha decided to take Sean to Kalpa, the main town of the area, but the hustle and bustle and crowds of even a small town did not appeal to me, and I decided to spend a quiet day reading on the veranda and generally pottering about. However, by mid-morning I was bored and decided to walk to the village of Chinie where the local tailor had promised to have a Kullu cap ready for me. I set off a little before noon and soon saw the flat roofs of the village huddled below.

Chinie is perched on a promontory high above the Sutlej river. The stone houses are squeezed together in a medieval jumble and the village is built around a path which winds up the hillside. In the centre of the village is a tiny square, and on the side of the square which overlooks the river is the temple, the largest building in the village, and easily the best kept. Built of pine and stone it is not as ancient as its traditional, Tibetan-influenced design suggests, but I was told that a temple had been on that spot for centuries.

I walked down the narrow lane flanked on each side by single-storey flat-roofed stone houses. I peered unashamedly into the dark interiors through the open doors. All the houses were empty, for in the summer almost all the life of the village is conducted outside. In the tiny village square women, children and a few men congregated each in their separate groups, all talking very loudly, the adults and older children busy with some chore. All smiled a greeting (even the women), and some yelled out, '*Namaste*,' taking great delight in the presence of a stranger, especially one who returned their greeting in Hindi. The children in particular were highly amused by my accent, and by the time I had entered the lane at the other side of the square I had a small crowd of them tugging on my clothing and laughing as I returned their '*Namaste*'. Each time I replied they would burst into fits of giggles. They followed me down the lane for about twenty yards, then, tiring of this game, they turned and ran back to the square.

The tailor was in one of the last buildings in the lane. Like all the shops in the village it consisted of a single room, about eight feet square, empty but for an old manual sewing machine. The tailor sat cross-legged on the steps of the shop, hand-sewing a shirt. He told me that my cap would not be ready for half an hour, and more in hope than in belief I decided to wait. I made my way back to the centre of the village. The novelty of the foreigner had worn off and I was spared the shouted greetings. I sat down near the gate of the temple but before I could get comfortable a kindly old man approached me and through gestures invited me into the temple yard. It was obvious he was keen to show me the inside of the temple, so I followed him in.

The temple was not grand, the grounds were not ornate; they were simply the rectangle in which the temple stood. This was not a tourist attraction like the one we had visited at Sarahan on our way to Kinnuer; this was a simple village temple, made mostly of wood. On the inside, the structure was remarkably similar to that of the Methodist chapel I had attended as a child. The contents were not. All around the inside of the temple small statues of Kali and Buddha were placed side by side; Kali, the Hindu goddess of destruction who drinks the blood of her victims, who inspires murderous cults, who demands blood sacrifices, and Buddha, the teacher of non-violence, peace and contemplation!

The statuettes were arranged next to each other on a shelf which ran round the walls of the room; first Buddha then Kali, thirty or so of each cast in bronze and in sparkling condition. On one side of the room there was a shrine with more of the Buddhas and a large framed print of his Holiness the Dalai Lama. On the other side of the room was a shrine to Kali with its statuettes, and a print of the goddess. This was one temple serving two totally different religions, both revered by the inhabitants of Chinie.

Outside I was shown the stone on which animals were sacrificed to Kali. A woman told me that the usual practice was to sacrifice them inside the temple but as a concession to the Buddhists in this village, they did it only in the temple yard. Of course, she added without a trace of irony, all religions are the same, only the form of worship differs. I said my goodbyes and, still struggling to come to terms with the apparent contradictions, walked out of the gate. There in front of me stood Sangratan, smiling his broad smile.

'Perplexed, Bill-*ji*?' he said.

'Very,' I said before clasping him in a warm embrace and blurting out how good it was to see him.

Even in the smallest village you can find a *chai* wallah and Chinie was no exception. I suggested we take some tea and he smiled and shook his head in agreement. I was at a bit of a loss as to what to say to him and almost began to mention the atrocious weather of the last few days but decided that drinking tea *and* talking about the weather would be far too English. I was full of questions as to where he had been, but Sangratan stated he was not keen to stay in the village, for 'large settlements make me uneasy.' (Since Chinie consists of not more than fifty houses I was surprised by his definition of a large settlement!)

We drank the tea quickly and in silence. Sangratan was grinning his broadest grin, and I could hardly contain my joy at seeing him again. Afterwards we walked down the lane and out of the village, passing on the way the tailor's shop where my Kullu cap was being made. The tailor was sitting with his friends chatting.

'Tomorrow,' he said sheepishly.

'Give him two more days,' said Sangratan, laughing.

Beside the track, just before it enters the village of Chinie, there is a large rock. There in the shadow of the rock sat Kirti. We sat down beside her. For a long time I talked and Sangratan listened. He asked me about my parents and I found myself recounting my life story. He listened patiently, interrupting only to seek clarification. When I had finished he was full of questions. 'What are computers?' 'Why leave your home and family to pursue work when you do not have to?' 'Why is it important to pursue a career?' 'Why is competition important to you?' and so on. All were asked gently, with great affection and a degree of wry amusement tempered with a degree of incredulity at my answers.

I asked him of his life and he told me that he was born near the Sangla valley close to the Sutlej river. He was one of four children but only he and his younger sister survived past early infancy. His father had been an Amchi. His parents died when he was very young and Sangratan and his sister were brought up by their uncle. He said they had travelled throughout the Kinnuer and regularly walked to Tibet, though since the occupation by China it was now much harder to travel freely. He told me he still went to Tibet every year before the snows came, but that each year it became more difficult. 'Times are changing faster than they used to,' he said. 'Soon there will be no more travelling Amchi. The land is being emptied, and the towns are being filled. There are new barriers everywhere. Even in this isolated area, the way of life is changing.'

He told me of his childhood. He was tutored by a 'lady of the Raj', the wife of an English official. As a young boy, when he wasn't helping his mother, he found work with this 'lady of great kindness' and it was she who taught him the English in which he was now so proficient. However, this friendship was to come to an end when his parents died, his uncle came for him and his nomadic life began.

He told me tales of his travels to Tibet when he was still a young child with his uncle and other relatives. The valley had been full of travellers in those days – merchants, smugglers, soldiers, pilgrims, monks and nomads. It was very exciting for a young boy. He described how they travelled into areas where 'the most violent of men' lived, of his fear and wonder at the skulls of their victims openly displayed in their villages. 'You see, Bill-*ji*, in the past these mountains produced the very best, and the very worst, of men. Men of kindness and men of casual cruelty living side by side,' he said. 'In these mountains are the descendants of those who collected as trophies the heads of others. In these mountains live men whose ancestors made human sacrifices, and here also live the descendants of some of the most gentle people the world has known.'

He explained that it had taken a long time for the people

of the mountains to learn how to live in harmony with each other. The temple in Chinie was a symbol of how different people have learned to live together. 'Tolerating that which you fundamentally disagree with is not an easy thing to do. It is not something which can be achieved without consistent and constant effort,' he said. He went on to explain that to live in harmony you need to develop your attitude so that tolerance is not a chore but comes effortlessly, a natural part of everyday life. But, according to Sangratan, tolerance is only the first step, for through tolerance we start to come closer together, and when we come closer together we recognise more easily the commonality of our hopes and dreams, and see much more than our differences. Sangratan says, 'An enemy has to be created and the way to start to make an enemy is to see only the differences between him and you. In times past there was a commonality of blood and group and a certain order encouraged by family and relatives. It was easier to live in peace in those days. Even now I think it is easier to be in this society, than in yours, Bill-ji. We had to learn that the differences between our kin and others were small and insignificant. The relationship between different people and the things of value that they pursue is the subject matter of the Third Lesson of Life.' This is what Sangratan then recounted to me:

The Third Lesson of Life tells us how to behave one to the other. It reminds us that we are social beings and that when we work together in harmony we achieve more. It also reminds us that we change and influence our world all the time, and the greater the harmony between all living things, even those things which can or do harm each other, the better for all. Indeed, the nurturing and development of those things that we cherish require that we are in agreement with others, for without agreement our tasks become so much harder and the outcome so much more unsatisfactory. In our pursuit of everything, we need to seek the agreement of those we value, if we are to develop it fully. The son who is not in agreement with his parents may do as they wish but his enthusiasm will be less. The younger brothers who disagree with their elder may still do his bidding, but with a heavier heart. The man who cheats another separates himself from the cheated and all who are close to his victim. He loses far more than the material gains his cheating brings. When we do not seek agreement we store up for ourselves a future without wholehearted effort, without genuine fraternity, and one with possible resentment and distrust.

Whereas the first two Lessons of Life help us to agree with ourselves those things which are important and how we should develop and nurture them, the Third Lesson of Life shows us that we should always seek as much agreement as possible with others before acting.

The Third Lesson of Life reminds us that because each one of us changes all of the time, there will always be differences between us, but by constantly seeking agreement we minimise the conflicts which continual change brings.

It is by seeking agreement with others that we begin to see that the differences between us are very small. Those who forget the Lessons of Life seek out and notice only differences between people, and between people and other sentient beings.

Often we are deluded into thinking that the differences between us and others are great. We take for granted our similarities and only see our differences, no matter how small. Often we hide behind our differences, the rich man forgetting that he is a poor man with wealth. Often, if we are very foolish, we try to accentuate these tiny differences. We see one small difference between us and another, and seek to create many others. We exclude that person from us simply on the basis of a single difference, and build more differences to keep him or her further away from us. For example, the rich lord uses his wealth and power to differentiate between himself and others by causing them to behave differently towards him than to each other. He accentuates differences by clothing, forms of address, access to land and property, possessions and goods. In this way he creates illusions which can lead only to false agreements, and is increasingly impoverished himself.

The Third Lesson of Life teaches us to look for the similarities between all living things, and to seek harmony with all. When we look at a tree and see it as different from us, our relationship with it is different than it would have been if we had seen the similarities between us and it. If we see only wood and leaves we will treat it differently than if we had seen it as one more living thing that, like us, stretches back through time, a living thing capable of reproducing itself and sensitive to changes in its environment, as we are to ours.

If a man can understand the feelings of others and all the ways in which they are alike, as a father, or mother, as a son, as a husband, as a worker, then he is far less likely to harm or want to harm, to kill or want to kill. The Buddhists, many Hindus, and others who live in these mountains know this lesson well, and when they look at cow or goat or any living creature they see another sentient being. When the non-violent worshipper in the temple at Chinie sees the blood sacrifice he may abhor the act, but he values the practitioner as another sentient being who shares with him most of the values and feelings that he has. Those who have learnt the Third Lesson well concentrate on that on which they can agree. Time and tolerance simply add to the accommodation one with the other.

The Third Lesson of Life also reminds us that we are thinking beings. We think and then we act. By sharing our thoughts with others and seeking their agreement, we help ourselves to see things more clearly and increase the possibility that our actions will be supported fully by those we value most. We also give others the opportunity to help us see the weaknesses in our plans and deliberations. Also, when we seek the agreement of others for our plans or actions we strengthen our own commitment both to what we plan to do, and to those from whom we seek agreement.

However, the Third Lesson of Life reminds us that animals and plants cannot give us their agreement, for our skills of communication are limited. In these cases we must try to imagine the consequences of our actions, and try to preserve what we imagine is their best interest. (We should also remember that, at times, we will make mistakes so we should always proceed with caution when dealing with decisions affecting other sentient beings.)

Once we have agreed a course of action with ourselves and with those close to us, we should act. Indeed, those who are to implement their plans successfully must ensure that there is no unnecessary delay between deciding and doing. Everything changes, everything has its rhythm. Decide, then act to plant corn in spring and you will eat well in winter; delay until summer and your crop will be consumed by winter snow! So it is with all actions, for it is very rare that situations resolve themselves, and a bad situation left alone usually gets worse.

Remember, life is work. We work to produce so many things – shelter, food, relationships, respect. Work is action. Thought should guide our action and not be an excuse for inaction. Only when we cannot think what to do should we do nothing! The Third Lesson reminds us that we should always find time to meditate, seek agreement and then act, and to do all three without unnecessary delays. For the nature of life is change and everything has its time.

There is one more aspect of the Third Lesson of Life, and it can be summarised thus: 'Be cautious in everything you do, but act without fear.' We need to remember this because it is in our nature to be wary of sudden change. We know that every day is a new day, and that most change is small and slow, but when we decide to nurture and develop what we value we often take what for us are big leaps into the unknown. We are like pilgrims on our first visit to a far-off shrine; we know others have been there before us but we are not sure of the way, or the hardships we will face, or what exactly awaits us when we reach our destination. We doubt ourselves and our abilities to cope with the journey. All this is natural. We are creatures of constant change, but the changes are very small, and very slow. It is difficult for us to seek out change, for what we know and are used to gives us comfort. Even if what we know and are used to damages us, we often have difficulty changing to more productive and satisfying ways and practices. In an ever-changing world we find reassurance in what was yesterday and is today even if it fails to satisfy us, even if it does us harm. We cling to tradition long after it has outlived its usefulness. We become afraid of what is new, afraid of change. For us effectively to pursue what we value, we have to relinquish the irrational fear of change. It is only by change that we achieve that which we value.

The wise man is not afraid, for he understands the nature of change. He knows life is not still. He constantly seeks to understand and adapt to his environment while conserving and developing what he values. He knows that he must constantly seek, constantly nurture, and knowing and accepting this imperative he is not fearful of change. He recognises and seeks to change, as he seeks all joy, for it is life. He is cautious, for he knows he needs to preserve and develop harmony, and he knows that agreement and harmony are built with small steps, not giant leaps. His pilgrimage is the pilgrimage of life, a pilgrimage of small steps to many different shrines, each containing what he values most. He meditates, seeks agreement, and moves, one step at a time, towards the shrine of what he values. And at each shrine he meditates, and then seeks agreement before moving on to the next shrine, on his pilgrimage of life.

7

The Philosophy of the Amchi

The morning was crisp and bright. The mountain peaks looked different again, reshaped by the snow that had come in the night. It was six in the morning, the day after my meeting with Sangratan in Chinie, and again I was setting out to meet him, with a sleeping bag, a thick shawl and a change of clothes. This time he had promised to teach me about the Amchi, and also allow me to travel with him when he visited those who needed his healing powers. I was excited at the prospect of seeing healing which had its roots in ancient philosophies, and which the Amchi had practised for hundreds of years. I was also keen to seek answers to scores of questions raised by Sangratan's expositions of the Lessons of Life.

As I reached the track, I turned and looked back at the farmhouse. Abha was standing at the door looking slightly forlorn. She raised her hand in farewell and I returned her gesture with as much vigour as I could muster. I walked on down the track, feeling guilty about leaving her and Sean alone while we were supposed to be on holiday together. I had sought her agreement and she had given it freely, but still both of us were saddened by the parting.

I glanced back from time to time as I walked on and saw that Abha stood watching. At a bend in the track I turned for the last time. She was standing, still and serene. She raised her hand again, and, smiling my bravest smile, I waved and walked on round the bend and out of sight. A few minutes apart and I already missed her. I made a mental note to ask Sangratan as to the nature of sadness which arises when agreement is freely given.

My sadness was slowly buried. The fresh morning air, the brisk exercise and the anticipation of a brand-new day with new experiences raised my spirits. The track climbed gently and entered the pine-scented forest that lined both sides of the valley, and the thick fragrance and morning birdsong helped to cheer me. At this point the forest was not very dense and birds of different sizes and colours flew from tree to tree and off out into the open sky above the river, often in pairs, calling and chattering as they darted this way and that.

I stopped and watched two Himalayan magpies speed in and out of the trees, flashing their splendid colours in the early morning sun. Playing, courting or hunting I knew not, but I remembered Sangratan's words about the power of small actions, and I imagined that it was in forests such as this, with their multitude of life and small activities, that humans first came to understand this power.

I pressed on. There was another sound that mingled with the sounds of the forest: the sound of panting. It came from my own overworked body as the incline became steeper, and the thin air made a mockery of my lowland, city-softened lungs. I started to think about the equipment I was bringing. Did I really need that shawl *and* the sleeping bag? Why did I bring the water bottle when everywhere the streams flowed with sweet, clean water? Gasping in great lungfuls of the thin air, and deep in thought about my accoutrements, I reached the top of the steep incline.

In front of me was a small depression about fifty metres wide, an oasis of green grasses in the middle of the forest. I stood and caught my breath. This was the spot, exactly as Sangratan had described it. Elated at being early and pleased at the chance of a rest, I sat down to wait for him. The morning sun was pleasantly warming and my sleeping bag made a very comfortable pillow as I lay down and closed my eyes. I lay there breathing deeply, relaxed and at peace.

Sometimes just before sleep, there is a point when you are filled with sensuous pleasure. You feel as if a great weight has been lifted from you, and you are beginning to float. It was as I was approaching that point that Sangratan and Kirti came noisily into the clearing.

'Ha, Bill-*ji*! Good, you are here,' he bellowed, overflowing with uncharacteristically boisterous good humour. 'Smell the air. It will be a fine day, full of new adventures and experiences,' he added, with far too much enthusiasm for an almost floating city-dweller.

'Hmmm,' I mumbled, stirring myself and slowly rising. '*Namaste-ji*, I said trying hard not to show any resentment.

He looked at my shawl, my sleeping bag, my toiletries, my torch and the change of clothes. 'I see you have come prepared,' he said with a broad smile.

Sangratan was wearing a Kullu cap. It was the first time I had seen him in one and it reminded me of how much taller than most of the local people he was. He wore his woollen shawl, which doubled as his bedding, wrapped around him as a kind of heavy *lunghi*.* From his shoulder hung a black cloth bag, and in his right hand he held a pine staff. He looked fit and powerful, every inch

---

* A cloth which men in south India wear wrapped round them instead of trousers, similar to the Scottish kilt.

the man of the mountains, while beside him stood Kirti, large and black, with her spiked collar gleaming in the early morning sun.

'Are we expecting leopards?' I asked, nodding towards the collar.

'No,' he said indulgently, 'leopards are shy creatures who only hunt at night. It is simply that Kirti must carry her own baggage, and this is the best way for her to do it.' I looked at Sangratan's small bag, aware that he was carrying all his worldly possessions, and started to gather up those I had brought. 'The day will be hot, Bill-*ji*, and the path is not an easy one. It is better to travel light,' he said.

I thought of the possessions I was carrying, my possessions back at the farmhouse, and my possessions back in Delhi. This is travelling light for me, I thought ruefully, and nodded agreement. Sangratan tapped his half-filled black bag. 'Medicines,' he said, and smiled. And so we started out, through the clearing and into the forest, Kirti, Sangratan the Amchi, and his overweight, over-burdened, city-dwelling follower.

Our path was steep, and getting steeper. Sangratan maintained a steady pace and I struggled to keep up. Occasionally, he would stop and wait for me and then we would stand looking down on where we had come until my breathing returned to normal and my thirst was quenched. At these resting points little was said. Sangratan stood and smiled his kindly smile, Kirti foraged ahead, and I gasped for breath. After a while, at one of these stops I realised that the forest had become much denser and was beginning to close in on the path. There was no grass here, for the ground was covered with a thick layer of dried, brown pine needles.

The birds had ceased to sing.

'We go this way,' Sangratan said, pointing into the forest, to the right of the path.

He started off. I followed. After a hundred yards or so I heard the sound of water, and a little later we came to a narrow stream of clear water, gushing and bubbling, rushing down the hill. The bed of the stream was covered in rocks and boulders, washed down from the heights. Sangratan pointed up the stream which mercifully ran at an angle to the main slope. 'Here is our path,' he said. 'The farm we seek is quite close.'

We pressed on, clambering over the boulders and rocks. Two hours later we came to the edge of the forest. In front of us was a clearing of scrub and thin short grass, strewn with boulders and rocks of every size and shape washed down from the steep valley sides. Sangratan stopped. He suggested we rest in the shade for the sun was high and there was little cover up ahead. I put down my load and sat with my back against a large tree. I had drained the water bottle during the trek, and Sangratan picked it up and filled it from the stream. He handed it to me but did not drink himself. When I had quenched my thirst, he refilled the bottle and handed it to me again; only then did he sit down.

'Today is the day you learn of the work of the Amchi,' he said. 'Soon we will be at the farm where he who needs us will be waiting, and you will see for yourself, but first you should know why we do what we do.' He then recounted to me the story of how the Amchi came to be. This is the story he told.

Though the Amchi have travelled the mountains for centuries, long before the time of the Buddha, it was not until the time of Tenzin that the true Amchi adopted all of the Lessons of Life. Tenzin was a Buddhist and incorporated much of Buddhism into the ways of the Amchi. In particular it was Tenzin who introduced the underlying Buddhist concept of 'mindfulness' into the Lessons of Life, though many claim that Buddha himself was the first Amchi.

All the Amchi know that the monk Gautama, before he became the Buddha, while he was still searching for 'the way', decided to practise severe austerities so that he could master physical desires, and in this way find enlightenment. It was common in those days, as it still is with certain holy people, to practise self-mortification in the hope of attaining a higher consciousness, and this is what he did. For many long months the monk Gautama subjected himself to all manner of deprivations and hardships. To overcome fear he sat alone at night in the darkest and most dangerous forests, full of leopards and ferocious bears. He practised holding his breath until his brain became inflamed. He went long periods of time without food or drink. He did not bathe, or cut his hair, or change his clothes. All day long he subjected his body to the unrelenting rays of the sun. He grew weak and his hair began to fall out. He was covered in dirt and dust, and his clothes turned to rags. He ate very little and then only discarded things, rotten husks, the dung of cattle. All the while he practised meditating.

One day he was meditating as darkness began to fall. The sun had been particularly cruel that day, blazing down unmercifully on the ragged, emaciated seeker of enlightenment. As it disappeared over the mountains, a cool breeze arrived to relieve his discomfort and refresh his tortured body. With the breeze and the relief came also the realisation that the mind and the body form one reality, and that to abuse the body was to abuse the mind. There and then the monk Gautama, he who became known as the Buddha, resolved to regain his health and use the joys of meditation to nourish and develop body and mind so that he could pursue the path of enlightenment. No longer did he wish to escape the world, but rather he realised that to gain enlightenment he should meditate on what he perceived, so that he could understand it better. He meditated on his body, on his feelings, on his perceptions and on his thoughts, and he saw the oneness of everything. He saw that as mind and body could not be separated, so all things were without a separate self. He saw that everything changed, and that impermanence and the emptiness of self are the very conditions necessary for life. He saw that a grass seed which was not impermanent and empty of self would never grow into a plant; it would simply remain static. Similarly with all things, including us. The monk Gautama, he who became Buddha, realised that everything was interdependent, everything was part of the oneness.

And the teachings of the Buddha influenced all who lived in these mountains be they Hindu, or of Bon,* or those that became the followers of the Buddha. All were influenced by his teaching, especially the Amchi, the ancient healers. All were changed in some way.

---

* The ancient religion of parts of the Himalayas, which includes Tibet. It pre-dates Buddhism.

The Amchi who existed before the Buddha did not understand the nature of impermanence nor of interdependence, and their practices reflected this. Many were ignorant of the balance of nature, and believed in the existence of demons who would enter and possess the bodies of the unwary or weak. Some would see illness or disease as a punishment from a god, or a penance for the sins of a previous existence. Sadly, some who call themselves Amchi, still do!

The true Amchi, the followers of Tenzin, learnt from the Buddha that to heal the body you must heal the mind, for they are one. Also, they know that a man or woman who is not in harmony with the environment and those around will continue to suffer dis-ease. The true Amchi seeks to create harmony and balance within the body, and with the body and what is perceived as the external world, for they are all one. So it is that all true Amchi attempt to bring harmony between all that is one.

The Amchi know that to exist we need to take into our bodies that which is outside, and let out that which is within. We are constantly doing this and constantly changing. We take in air, and heat and cold, and plants and fruits, and minerals, and fluids and gases, and thoughts and experiences, and many different minute life-forms, and we change them as they change us, and then we let these changed entities out. The true Amchi understands this process and seeks to balance what is taken in, what is within, and what is given out. And they do this through plants, oils and medicines, and good counsel and teaching.

The herbs and other plants and oils remind us of what we are, and what we need, and what we will be, and the other medicines also do this. Often these medicines are created by men and they are made in the peace and harmony which comes through chanting and meditating. When we take them they change and pass through us, as we change and pass through the world and the universe.

To overcome sickness we need to live in harmony and balance with the world around us, especially those things and people we value highly. To be free of dis-ease we must seek to balance that which is within, as we seek to balance that which is not. For all affect us as we affect everything, for we are all one.

The Amchi's counselling and teaching seeks to help us live in balance and harmony. We know that to thrive we must not be too hot or too cold, too hungry or too thirsty, too empty or too full. We know also that conflict, anxiety, fear, despair, jealousy, anger, sadness, hate, separation from those whom we value highly, all these things bring dis-ease and suffering. It is for the Amchi, the healer, to help restore the harmony of body and mind, and the world, and to bring peace and joy; and to do this we have to help those who are suffering from dis-ease to be mindful of that which they value, and mindful of what they seek to develop and nurture. The Lessons of Life are the practical application of the Amchi's art in seeking to harmonise the person with his or her oneness.

Sangratan stopped speaking. He closed his eyes and sat perfectly still. Sitting cross-legged, his forearms resting on his knees, he was meditating. I sat silently watching him, noting the half smile on his serene face. Long minutes passed, Sangratan continued to meditate. I thought about getting up and stretching my legs but felt nervous about disturbing him. I sat and waited. Finally he opened his eyes and smiled. He seemed to glow with happiness.

'This man we are going to meet, he is not a follower of the Buddha,' he said. 'He is influenced by his place in the universe. He is typical of those we seek to help, for this is a meeting place of many great ideas and cultures. These ideas come and are changed by those experiencing them, as all ideas and teachings are changed, for they are as impermanent as all things. We Amchi counsel that they meditate on what they value, knowing that being mindful of what they value will bring understanding, and understanding defeats ignorance and brings love, and love will bring nurturing, and nurturing will bring joy, and joy is the end of suffering. So, understand that when we attempt to heal someone who is suffering we seek not only to balance the body but to help balance that sentient being with all. Do not see only the herbs and medicines. Do not hear only the words. See the suffering and see all the ways we seek to ease the suffering and bring joy to all.'

There was another long silence. Again, I did not know what to say. Sangratan was looking at me like a loving father looks upon a small child. I was overwhelmed with a feeling of love and acceptance. I luxuriated in it, savouring the joy which comes from being loved and accepted. He stood and, extending his arms, reached out and grabbed my forearms and helped me to my feet. He held my arms for a moment and, smiling, studied my face.

'Come,' he said. 'Not far now.'

8

Love

Within twenty minutes we were standing outside the door of a stone hovel, a dilapidated dwelling with a flat earth roof and two tiny windows. It was situated on the edge of the clearing against the slope of the valley side. The occupant had collected some of the stones and small boulders which were strewn around the clearing and made two untidy piles at the side of the house. I guessed they were materials for repair. Unlike the houses of people lower down the valley, this one did not have a black plastic water tank or a feed from the stream. No running water. No electricity. The door had once been painted green but now it had peeled and flaked and the bare wood was exposed.

Sangratan said something in the local dialect and pushed the door open. I peered into the dark interior as he walked in, my eyes adjusting to the gloom. This was the house of a very poor person. It was dark and damp. The floors of the single room were without stone flagging or a concrete base; the walls were unadorned and black with dirt, grease and soot. Light was shining through the gaps between the stones in three or four places. Along the far wall was a high shelf. On it rested one blackened and battered cooking pan. In the far corner, a tattered frayed print of Shiva, torn from a calendar, clung to the wall, the legend 'December 1989' proclaiming its vintage. On the near side of the room on a ragged blanket spread on the ground lay what at first glance I took to be a scrawny old man. However, I quickly realised that he was young, no older than thirty, unwashed and with skin the texture and colour of oiled leather. He was under-dressed for the coolness of the room in trousers and vest, without shoes or socks. Dirt was engrained on his ankles. The trousers were held in place around the waist by cord that once had been white. He sat up as Sangratan entered the room with hands brought together in greeting. The young man did the same and Sangratan sat cross-legged beside him. I stayed in the doorway, for in this room three would have been a crowd.

Without saying a word, Sangratan took the man's wrist and felt his pulse. Then he placed his palm on the man's forehead, and when satisfied went back to taking his pulse. After another minute or so he told the man to lie down, and ran his palm gently over the man's abdomen and chest. Again he went back to the pulse-taking. There then began a conversation between them in the local language, accompanied by so much smiling and nodding of the head that it was impossible for me to guess at the content of Sangratan's inquiries or the man's responses. All the while Sangratan's hands were busy, at one moment placed gently on a shoulder, the next squeezing a forearm, pressing a leg, turning a hand to examine the nails. Finally Sangratan turned to me. 'This is Ananda,' he said, 'and he needs you to get him some water in that fancy bottle of yours.' Ananda smiled a broad smile, his thin face retreating behind a mouthful of protruding teeth. I smiled, nodded and turned quickly in the direction of the stream.

The house was about fifty yards from the stream, far enough away to escape the monsoon and snow-melting inundations. The route to the stream was strewn with boulders and rocks, making it a time-consuming hundred yards. By the time I returned

Ananda was lying on his front, naked to the waist. Sangratan was rubbing oil from a very small bottle on to Ananda's scrawny neck, talking to him in a low voice. Again I could not understand what was being said and I felt I was intruding. I put down the water bottle and went outside.

It was then that I noticed a young man sitting quietly at the side of the house. His face wore an expectant smile, and I realised he had been watching me, waiting a long time for me to notice him. I brought my palms together in greeting, and walked towards him. He looked like a much younger, healthier version of the man in the house.

'*Bhai*,'* I said, motioning towards the door.

'*Hanji*,'† he said, a weak smile quickly appearing and disappearing from his face.

'Don't worry, OK,' I said, my Hindi failing me, and I smiled what I thought was a reassuring smile.

My new acquaintance did not look reassured. I introduced myself and he told me his name was Raju, and there followed a laboured conversation as his Hindi was almost as poor as mine. I did manage to ascertain that he was the younger brother, his mother was expected back any moment, and his brother Ananda had been sick a long time. 'Stomach problems,' he implied through sign language.

We sat and looked down at the valley. Raju became quicker to smile, and a common system of gestures and single Hindi words allowed us to communicate. Raju was keen to show

---

* Hindi: 'Brother.'
† Hindi: 'Yes, sir.'

hospitality to a guest but, since this was a poor family, his kindness manifested itself in offers of water to drink and much exhorting for me to try ever more comfortable places to sit. Just when I thought he had exhausted his offers, a tiny woman of middle years walked into the clearing. It was Raju's and Ananda's mother, Sita.

Raju introduced us, we said *Namaste*, and she began another round of offering to fetch water and proposing new sitting places. She was dressed in a floral-printed yellow-and-green Salwar Kameeze and dark brown, torn cardigan, which was a little too small for her, buttoned at the neck. On her head she wore a Kullu cap. Her only ornaments were a plain gold ring and a white bead necklace. Her face was scrubbed and shiny and glowing, and her hair oiled and tied back in one long plait. Her body was slight and tough, honed by years of hard labour in the fields. Crows' feet around her eyes betrayed her age, but she had a ready smile, and quick, sparkling eyes. I sensed that she must have always looked this way, for she seemed to wear the hardships lightly.

Her Hindi was a lot better than her son's, and her questions direct and good-humoured. Was I a *Gori?** Why did I have a brown head? Where was I from? Was I an Amchi? How did I come to be with the Amchi? Was I very rich? How much did I earn? Did I have much land? Did I have a cow? – 'You have all that money and you don't have a cow?' All these questions and many more were asked for curiosity's sake, without envy or agenda. Soon we were laughing together for she found amusement in everything, her dark eyes flashing with childlike

---

* Hindi: white.

pleasure in new company. Time passed.

Sangratan came out of the house. Sita's face lost its smile. Pleasantries were exchanged but there was tension in her expression and Raju went very quiet and stared hard at the ground. Sangratan and Sita talked softly in the local dialect. After a short while they walked to the stream where Sangratan slaked his thirst. Then they returned to the house.

Another half hour passed. Raju and I sat and waited. Finally Sangratan, Sita and Ananda walked out of the house. Ananda now looked a little better. 'It is time for us to leave,' said Sangratan, and we swiftly said out goodbyes. Sita bent to touch Sangratan's feet in blessing, but he anticipated and, taking hold of her shoulders, stopped her. She gazed up at him with a weak smile and he gave her his most radiant one in return.

The two young men made half-hearted attempts at touching Sangratan's feet, both of which Sangratan easily thwarted. I said my goodbyes, shaking hands with the men, bringing my palms together for Sita. Sita produced a small bag of rice, enough for an evening meal, and gave it to Sangratan who, accepting it graciously, placed it in his black cloth bag. Kirti stirred herself from her shady hideaway, and the three of us walked off, back down the trail in the direction we had come.

'Well?' I said, as soon as we were out of earshot. 'What's the story there?'

'I'll explain in a short while,' said Sangratan, and walked on with slow, measured steps, breathing softly and rhythmically, his eyes sparkling and with a broad smile on his features. He was enjoying the exercise and its effect on his body, the forest, the birds, the butterflies, the slight breeze, the fragrances, the heat of the sun's rays. He was alive to everything and it registered on his face. I walked beside him in silence. Once I found a rhythm in my breathing, I too began to gain greater joy from the surroundings, and as Sangratan's 'short while' stretched into the second hour, I put Ananda, Raju and Sita to the back of my mind, and began to savour the forest, the walk and our silence.

The sun was beginning its descent as Sangratan came to a halt and suggested we rest for a while. I put down my pack and sat against the nearest tree. Looking up I realised that the forest was changing. Here other trees mingled among the pine, and up ahead they dominated the hillside.

'We'll soon be at our evening resting place,' said Sangratan.

Refreshed, I asked, 'Tell me about Ananda.'

'This was the first time I had met him,' he replied. 'Raju came to see me the day before yesterday, and told me that Ananda was suffering. He is a good boy, Raju, strong and compassionate. His mother will be pleased to have such a son in her old age.'

'And will she be pleased with Ananda as well?' I asked. Sangratan paused, and then looking directly at me said, 'Ananda is like many people, absorbed by himself and by "possessing". For him even love is a possession. He is suffering because he is abusing his body and mind. In the process he is causing suffering to his mother and his brother and almost all who come into contact with him. He is in need of much healing.'

Sangratan looked at me, waiting for me to speak. The smile had left his face. I remembered how Sangratan had behaved with Ananda, offering him friendship, caring and concern, the two of them laughing and conversing. 'But you were so friendly and concerned for him,' I said.

Sangratan's smile returned. 'I am an Amchi, and a sentient creature like him. He is suffering, of course I am concerned,' he said quietly.

'In what way is he suffering?' I asked, confused by Sangratan's attitude.

'Ananda is not mindful of what he values. He has forgotten the First Lesson of Life. He does not meditate on what he values, and so he is obsessed with himself. Because of this he ignores the Second Lesson of Life, which is to develop and nurture that which he values, and he also ignores the Third Lesson, which is to seek agreement with those close to him, in his case, his mother and Raju. It is very basic with him. He is suffering in his values, his family, and his body.' Sangratan paused, his face unsmiling. Kirti raised herself and moved close, sitting down beside him and placing her head on his thigh. I waited for Sangratan to continue.

'Ananda's physical symptoms are chronic acidity, malnourishment, stomach and bowel disorder, slight kidney and liver damage, and spondylosis,' he said in a dispassionate tone. 'The acidity, stomach, bowel, kidney and liver problems are related to his drinking large quantities of *chung*,* as is the malnourishment, but that is also related to material poverty. The spondylosis is due to the harsh nature of the labour that the poor around here have to subject themselves to. The drinking of large quantities of *chung* is a symptom of his estrangement from his values. It is an expression of

---

* The local alcohol.

his obsession with what he erroneously considers to be his "self". He is suffering because he sees himself as a separate entity from his environment, his mother and his brother.' At last Sangratan's smile returned. 'To ease his suffering I have given him some medicines, to disperse his suffering I have told him to meditate on what he really values, and to meditate on the value of *chung!* When he meditates on both with an open mind he will find what he truly values and pursue it. Ananda needs to find the loving kindness and compassion to remove his mother's and brother's suffering, and when he does he will ease his own suffering, for we are all interdependent. To find this loving compassion it is necessary for him to meditate on the nature of love, and on his love for his mother and brother.

'I have given him instructions on what and how to meditate. First he must meditate on his values and when he has them clear, he should meditate on what love is based. In sequence he must consider what is love? Does he love his mother? Why does he love his mother? How should he demonstrate love? In all this he will discover that love is something which is given but cannot be owned. It is not permanent, as everything is impermanent. It is given today and it needs to be given tomorrow, for it has no existence outside the giving. Love is constantly being made and constantly being given. It can be accepted, but it cannot be owned. Words can demonstrate love, but it requires action as well as words to manifest itself. Love is not empty words but kindness and compassion.

'Ananda must learn that love is also selflessness. Usually when people think of love they think that love exists in relationships of ownership. "My" love. People want only to love that to which they "belong" or which "belongs" to them. "My parents", "my relatives", "my wife", "my children", "my people", "my country". This possessive emotion, based on discrimination, breeds prejudice, and is a source of suffering for ourselves and others. Ananda, if he meditates correctly, will understand that the reasons that exist to love his mother are there in all mothers, and in all fathers and in all sentient beings who nurture and develop others. He will learn that the qualities which he loves in his brother exist in all brothers and sisters, and in all beings which grow and develop interdependently. And when he is truly enlightened he will see the interdependence of *all* living things, and the qualities within them which loving kindness and compassion nurture and develop.

'And if Ananda meditates on *chung* he will see its real value, and he will not imbibe as much, if at all. I expect him to see the value in his mother and brother and see how his drinking *chung* is hurting them all. I will return to ensure that Ananda reaches agreement about his drinking or non-drinking with his mother and brother, and begins to give some loving kindness and compassion to them.'

Sangratan sat with his eyes closed as if in his head he was playing back the words he had just spoken. There was a stillness and a quietness about him for what seemed like a long time, then he opened his eyes and smiled his most heart-warming smile. Kirti silently stood up and sauntered off to explore the forest.

Sangratan put his hands into his black cloth bag and withdrew a smaller bag made of newspapers containing a little bottle of dark oil. Pointing to the oil he said, 'Ayurvedic, excellent for the spondylosis. I gave a bottle like this to Sita to apply to Ananda. It will bring them closer and cure his neck.' He withdrew another newsprint bag of small brown pellets bearing a remarkable resemblance to rabbit droppings. 'Magic medicines,' he said with a chuckle, and for a moment I thought he was joking and that they were some kind of placebo that he had given Ananda. 'Made on auspicious nights by chanting monks,' he said, and I realised he was serious.

'Magic?' I asked.

'The magic is in the mindful chanting,' he said seriously. 'They are made with selfless love, compassion and care. It is this which gives them their healing properties. For they are made by people in active agreement and unison. The medicinal qualities they get from their ingredients. They will balance Ananda's body.'

Sangratan had finished his discourse. Without saying another word we got up and walked on in silence. I thought of the monks who had so diligently made the medicines with collective compassion, seeking the best time according to their calendar. I thought of Sangratan administering to Ananda, helping him to examine more closely what he valued, and seek agreement about how to develop and nurture it. I thought of how Raju had sought out Sangratan, and of the small bottle of oil that was left for Ananda's mother to ease her son's discomfort and bring them closer together. I thought of their poverty and hardship, and the small bag of rice she gave, and her joy in the giving. I hoped that Ananada would understand the nature of loving kindness and compassion, and the joy they bring to the person giving. I thought of myself and hoped that I could throw off the conditioning of my own society which saw giving and receiving as a mutually balanced exchange, and love as a possession, used to exclude others. I thought of the joy that came from giving loving kindness and compassion without expectation of return. As we walked Sangratan was smiling his usual smile, and I realised that now I too was smiling.

9

Sangratan the Healer

Up ahead was the farmhouse where we would spend the night, its corrugated metal roof gleaming under the evening sun. We had descended into a tributary valley of the Sutlej, and the last few hundred yards had been easy walking through pasture and apple and almond orchards. The sun was sinking and the sky was beginning to turn red. The air was fresh and the temperature ideal for the light exertion of our downhill walk. We were walking a well-worn, dusty path, far easier on the legs and feet than the rocky stream path we had traversed earlier. I felt good.

The farmhouse looked particularly inviting. It was well kept with a small neat herb garden near the door. No peeled and cracked woodwork here, but solid pine frames, doors and windows. A fresh coat of pale green paint on the walls and the shininess of the roof indicated recent renovation. The well-laid-out orchard in front of the house attested to the care and hard work of the occupants. Buddhist prayer flags hung limply on poles arranged symmetrically round the house. There were stone steps leading from the path up to the house, and the fresh mortar which held them in place proclaimed the wealth of the farm-owners. Now we were near enough to see that there were in fact two identical dwellings adjoining one another to house an extended family.

As we approached, two large brown dogs came running down the path, barking and growling. Kirti stopped, her head held high, a low growl coming from her slightly open mouth. The dogs pulled up in front of her. They too began a low growling, and in turn they walked up to her, placed their neck upon the back of hers, growled some more and, satisfied, took turns at sniffing and being sniffed. 'She knows them,' said Sangratan.

The three dogs walked quickly ahead in single file, and we followed. As we approached, a welcome party came out and formed up in a line in front of one of the doors. Adults and children all wore traditional caps, and the children wore soft green jackets over their robes. The very small children, a girl and boy, fidgeting and giggling, alternately looked down at the ground and then up at me, holding hands in excited nervousness.

An old woman took one step forward, an expression of love and gratitude on her face, struggling to find words. Sangratan took her hands in his, and gazed deep into her eyes. For a long moment nothing was said while the old lady gently rocked back and forth. Then Sangratan let go and very gently cupped her face in his hands. Tears welled up in her eyes and she smiled, a greeting without words.

Sangratan walked down the line, holding each face in his hands, warmth and affection on his face. He crouched low in front of the children, and as they buried their chins on their chests, he kissed the top of their heads. Finally, when all had been silently greeted, he introduced me.

The matriarch was named Sujata. She was still strong and active with a fresh complexion, and only the prominent veins and wrinkled translucent skin on the back of her hands betrayed her age. She was wrapped in a traditional long woollen robe, held at the waist with a narrow crimson sash. She smiled and nodded at me, offering the warm welcome for which the people of this valley are renowned.

Her son Sanjay was approaching thirty-five years of age but, unlike his mother, he had retained the shyness of one who had lived long in a small, enclosed community. A tall, broad-shouldered man, he was dressed in his best western clothes: trousers, shirt and a red jersey. Beside him stood his wife, Nandini. Short, with almond eyes, high cheekbones and black hair parted on the side, she too wore an ankle-length robe and over it a soft grey woollen cardigan. She had the same direct and open look as her mother-in-law. Self-confident women abound among the Kinnar.

Nandini's son Rajiv, all of five years old, stood smiling beside his mother, without a trace of his father's shyness. He too was dressed in his best clothes, his robe tied with a thin cloth belt. His younger sister, Sangita, wore a similar outfit, but the bottom of her robe was decorated with an elaborate abstract patterned border, and the cuffs of her soft green jacket were decorated with red velvet.

Beyond the flowerbeds chairs had been arranged in a semi-circle, and Sujata beckoned us to sit. No sooner had we done so than Nandini brought a small table and placed it in front of us, and moments later we were being served hot sweet masala *chai*. Sangratan placed his cup on the table, and then accompanied Sujata into the house. Again I was being smothered with kindly hospitality as each member of the family sought to provide a welcome fit for an honoured guest. But not for long. Sangratan appeared at the door and gestured for me to join him.

Inside was a neat room with a concrete floor. There were

signs of wealth: a hand-made multi-striped rug and a low double bed, a straight-backed chair, and new brown curtains around the single window. Sitting on the bed was an old man, Sujata's husband. Obviously in pain, he was bent over trying to bring some relief to his lower abdomen. In his hand was a small metal pot. Sangratan introduced him as Shiv Saran and a quick smile came and went, momentarily replacing his grimaces of pain.

Sangratan took the metal pot from him, looked at its contents for a long moment, and finally dipped his finger in and tasted the contents. He put the pot down and as he did so I realised that it contained Shiv Saran's urine. Sangratan raised an eyebrow in query as my face registered my thoughts. I looked away.

Sangratan took Shiv Saran by the wrist and took his pulse. He was silent, concentrating hard. After a while he let go of the wrist, and with a soft low groan Shiv Saran rolled over and lay down in the foetal position on the bed.

Sangratan looked at me. 'You are shocked Bill-*ji*? That the Amchi tastes the urine of his patient?'

'Not really,' I lied.

'Nor should you be,' he said. 'I am told that where you come from they put dead animals, and far more dreadful things in their mouths.'

I remained silent, chastened.

Sangratan went back to examining Shiv Saran, gently pressing the old man's lower abdomen, and taking his pulse over and over again. Through it all Shiv Saran was stoical, his closed eyes, the occasional grimace and the odd involuntary groan the only signs of the excruciating pain he was suffering. Sangratan asked him many questions until he was finally satisfied. He turned to me.

'It is a serious business, Bill-*ji*,' Sangratan said, in English. 'He has many disorders, all of them to do with the small changes which we call ageing, but one which could be fatal in the very near future. He has a hot disease in the abdomen and as you can see he is suffering greatly. From reading his pulse I can tell that the wind energy in his body is out of balance.'

My ignorance must have shown on my face for Sangratan went on to explain the medicinal beliefs of the Amchi. There are 'winds' which circulate inside the body, four flows of energy that, like everything else, must be kept in balance. Too much wind affects the marrow in the bones, and the acidity of the blood. An imbalance affects the digestive and reproductive organs, kidneys, heart and lungs. When there is too much of one type of energy flow it affects the muscles, as does too little. All diseases are classified by the Amchi as 'hot' or 'cold' or 'neutral' diseases, so for instance you could have hot, cold or neutral arthritis. Cure is dependent on the patient, the medicine and the environment, in the sense of diet, where the patient lives, and how he is prepared to make changes in the way he lives.

The Amchi dispense medicine, advise on diet, on the way to live, and on changes in the immediate environment. This often means advising the family as to what has to be changed. The Amchi know that suffering is eased by small actions and that full recovery can take months or even years. They know that those with mental strength and will-power will recover faster, and they encourage meditative practices to strengthen the mind and thought processes.

They know that being compassionate, kind and fearless aid recovery, and that relaxing and enjoying the company of others is very important if disease is to be overcome.

Sangratan explained that Shiv Saran had a variety of ailments and that his energy flows were greatly out of balance. His body with its immune systems weakened by age and the accumulation of many long-present small diseases, was suffering in most of its functioning. Sangratan believed that the 'hot' disease in his abdomen could prove fatal. 'However, he is very strong, and his body may be able to produce energy to counter this hot disease,' he added.

While he spoke he reached into his bag and took out five round brown pills, each about a quarter-inch in diameter. 'These are the last of this medicine that I have, and it is a long walk and many weeks before I can replace them. But their time has come. These are the most effective medicines of Tibet. The monks who make them claim they can help cure any ill. I know that they have been effective many times with serious disease. Let us hope they help now, for without these I believe Shiv Saran will not last long in this form.'

We moved back to the bedside. Sangratan spoke in the local dialect to Shiv Saran, a short exchange which ended in laughter.

'I told him it looked serious,' Sangratan explained. 'He said, for me it also feels serious!' Shiv Saran was smiling weakly.

Sangratan stepped outside, and spoke softly to each family member, not words of reassurance that everything would be fine, but of reaffirmation that life was taking its course; a gentle reminder to meditate on the nature of disease, and life and death, instructions as to what to do to ease Shiv Saran through this night. Painkilling and anti-inflammatory medicines, both Ayurvedic and Tibetan, were produced from Sangratan's black bag, and instructions given about dosage.

The most potent medicine in Sangratan's possession – the tablets from Tibet – was to be given one hour before sunrise. Before sleeping, Sujata was to put a pellet into a cup of water so that it would dissolve overnight. The next morning Shiv Saran was to drink the concoction, and then return to bed and cover himself with as many blankets as he could bear. He must stay there, fully covered, for at least one hour. Five pellets, five days, starting the next morning. Sangratan found a task for each family member, giving each the chance to administer to the old man and to express loving concern, kindness and compassion. The mood of those in the house lifted. Shiv Saran drifted into fitful sleep, helped by kindly ministrations and the medication.

The sun disappeared and the sky grew dark. Kerosene lamps were lit and bathed the rooms and veranda in soft brown light. In the kitchen the glow of embers combined with the lamp light to produce golden walls and soft shadows. We sat on the veranda with the door open so that we could keep watch on the ailing Shiv Saran. Small tables were placed in front of us and steel *thalis** laid on them. Before us stretched the bright moonlit sky, the soft shadows of forest on the far side of the valley, and the blue, eerie, whiteness of the snow-covered tops. A few small clouds

---

* Plates with raised edges.

scurried away, clearing the sky for thousands of stars.

We ate *dal*, rice and spicy pickles; basic but filling, and very welcome after the exertions of the day. We ate in a silence that I later realised was the custom with this family and many others in the valley who had been brought up to meditate on the preciousness of the food that they consumed. After the meal Sujata went and sat with her ailing husband who was dozing but still in great pain, his eyes and cheeks looking hollow in the yellow shadows of the lamp-lit room.

Outside his door, life went on. Sangratan regaled us with stories of his travels. The children's eyes widened as he told of his meetings with leopards, and his adventures on distant passes as the snows closed in around him. Children and parents were engrossed in his words. I watched their faces and was grateful for an explanation of the storyline in English every so often. From Sangratan's expressions I could see he was making them as dramatic as possible for the children's enjoyment – a master storyteller seeking to entertain and teach.

The children's stories ended, and local hooch was brought out in an ancient bottle, full of clear distilled spirit, looking like water, but smelling strong enough to strip paint. I sniffed at the open neck. 'The people of this valley like to drink strong liquor,' Sangratan said, 'but be warned, Bill-*ji*, even they drink this diluted with water.' The tingling in my nostrils had already made me decide to give this potent brew a miss, but I was the only adult to do so. All the others, including Sangratan, heartily imbibed and, despite the illness of the sleeping Shiv Saran, the mood of the household became very jolly.

We had been allocated a room with two beds. It was comfortable, clean, spartan. As we prepared our bedding the contradictions of the evening came to mind. I asked about the Buddhist flags around the house and the Hindu names of the occupants. I asked about enjoying alcohol after seeing Ananda earlier in the day. And I asked about the mixing of medicines from Tibet and India, from two distinct and separate cultures and philosophies with different approaches to life.

This is what Sangratan answered.

Many of the people of this valley, like many in this land, adopted and adapted the nuances and practices of other religions. They did not discard the old religions, but simply added aspects of other religions to their existing practices. History is full of such instances. That is why the same religion may have many different aspects, belief systems and rituals, varying from place to place and from time to time.

This family are Hindu, and they believe in Hindu gods. Their ancestors were probably converts from Bon for they also believe in the gods of the village, and in Tantric practices. Their neighbours who are Buddhists believe that the writing on the flags promotes well-being. Sujata's family thinks that the Buddhists' good fortune may have something to do with the flags, so why not adopt this practice?

Some inhabitants of the valley still cling to the Tantric ways of the old local religion, but they adopt and adapt Hindu worship and Buddhist practices. As I have said, Bill-*ji*, you must

understand the interdependence of men, women and all living
things. I have not seen other lands but I know that it is the same
everywhere. We all influence each other. You Christians have so
many festivals and practices adapted and incorporated from
different religions. So it is with all religions and all beliefs.

The people living in this area have learnt to accept the
new, often without rejecting the old. They accept in search of
harmony. They accept for acceptance's sake. That which is
beyond our control, we have to accept. Consider. Hindus now
believe in astrology, which was not originally part of their
religion – they acquired it from the Greeks. The Buddha was a
Hindu who adapted and included many aspects of Hinduism and
found a 'new way'. In this valley Buddhists still cling to many
Shaman practices. Both Hindus and Buddhists still keep the local
deities and ritualistic practices of more ancient times, and more
ancient belief systems. All religions change as everything changes,
and it does not matter, as long as peace and harmony are
nurtured.

So it is even with the Amchi. Tenzin, the collector of the
Lessons of Life, was a Buddhist from Tibet, but the Lessons of
Life are an amalgamation of mostly ancient Sanskrit and
Buddhist writings collected so that, whatever the religious beliefs
of the sufferer, the Amchi could give practical relief to suffering.
There are texts which we study to help us heal. There are the
Lessons of Life that we study so that we can advise and help
people to find the way to minimise suffering. The true Amchi
studies the Lessons of Life, and all the sutras, and the ancient
Tibetan texts and manuscripts. The intermingling of people and

ideas and practices and all that you see around you, Tibet and
Bharat, Buddhist and Hindu, are the result of the need to develop
harmony, and relieve suffering.

The Amchi of Tibet are different from the Amchi here,
for they travel regular short distances. The Amchi who are
followers of Tenzin travel long distances and draw from many
philosophies, Hindu and Buddhist, Christian and Confucian. We
Amchi who follow Tenzin hold to old ideas and philosophies
but judge their validity against our lives. If the old ideas are
found wanting, we change, reshape or discard them. In this way
we change ourselves and our ideas, and our environment. We use
Ayurvedic medicines because they help us ease the suffering that
faces those who need our help. We are taught to live in the
present, as we teach others to live in the present. We know that
since all things change, so do our tools and our methods. We
keep with us that which we have learnt because of its continued
utility, as we adopt different methods if we see utility in them.
We shed that which no longer has great value, as the things we
value change or the means to what we value changes. We cling to
the Lessons of Life because they still have great utility. Like birth
and death, they are a constant of human existence, and in that
sense they are permanent as long as life as we know it is
permanent. They have a new birth in each person who comes to
them.

Understand this. The Amchi see suffering almost every
day. Life here is very hard. Children are born and their mothers
die. Children grow and often do not reach adulthood. We all
change, age and die. Our lives are small, our actions smaller. We

are minute parts of the river of life, coming together, going apart, endlessly rejoining, reforming. Our suffering lies in our attachment to this constantly changing cosmic existence, but so does our joy. We must savour and nurture our attachment, but accept that we will all eventually become detached. The Ancients in all lands understood this. They knew that compassion and kindness bring joy and ease suffering. And they knew that approaches to living had to be formulated and written down. From biblical times, from the time of Confucius, Jesus, Buddha, from Vedic times, men have written down ways to behave.

The Amchi, those who dedicate their lives to healing, draw from the Lessons of Life, for their utility continues to this day. Each Amchi meditates and examines new thoughts, ideas, relationships. They walk old paths, and see them anew. They walk new paths and see how the actions of the past have shaped and formed them. Like all people, the Amchi seek joy and a life without suffering. They do not consume large quantities of alcohol or anything which disturbs the balance of their being, but they do not advocate abstinence. Drink too much *chung* and you will suffer for it. One drink may improve your balance, four drinks may destroy it. Eat too many apples and you will suffer dis-ease. A few apples are good for you; fifty or sixty a day and you will have a host of problems!

The Lessons of Life also teach us that, despite our best efforts, from time to time changes will occur that bring suffering: the violent storm which destroys crops or causes a landslide; the minute creature which throws our system out of balance, causing us extreme pain and other symptoms of dis-ease; the changes we call ageing; a host of situations caused by the behaviour of others over which we have no control; the suffering of bereavement, of betrayal, of disease, of debilitating injury – all cause suffering which we cannot avoid. The Lessons of Life teach us that 'that which we cannot change we must understand', for understanding removes ignorance, and it is the removal of ignorance which lessens the suffering and strengthens us.

Consider. Shiv Saran is near to death. He has been here before. I do not tell Sujata not to worry, all will be all right; I tell her to meditate on death.* I ask her to consider where death occurs, and where it does not occur. I ask her to consider when it occurs, and when it does not occur. I ask her to consider what and who death involves and what and who it does not involve. These aspects she must consider if she is to understand death, for in the understanding, ignorance is dispelled and suffering eased.

Here, tonight, you saw that this family understands the suffering which comes with illness, and they also understand what it means to live with bereavement – one of their sons has already died. They have meditated on, and understand the nature of life and the nature of death. They know that death is part of all life. They have learnt to live in the present, and they understand that possessiveness is destructive. If a person they value is no more, they are thankful for the joy that that person brought. They regret the passing, and feel the sorrow, but they understand the nature of the change and live with it, without the greater sorrow that possessiveness and ignorance bring.

---

* See Appendix II

Throughout the night they will be expressing loving kindness in a variety of ways, taking turns providing comfort and care for the ailing Shiv Saran. Even the small children will sleep little tonight, but they will not grieve as the possessive grieve. Their lives go on as normal with the extra tasks that Shiv Saran's illness gives them. They are concerned, but not worried. They are hopeful, but realistic. They do not despair about what has not occurred, nor will they be unprepared if death comes. They have learnt the Lessons of Life well. They will be saddened by their loss, but understand its nature and its place in the scheme of things.

———————◆———————

Sangratan fell silent. He sat in the lotus position, upright and still, the light from the moon full upon him. I looked at him, silent, not wanting to break the spell of the night. I sensed the power of his concentration filling the room. In the moonlight he seemed to glow. I was transfixed as he radiated calmness and compassion. In a moment he had transformed himself from a lively sociable companion to a mystical philosopher sage.

The room seemed suddenly brighter. I could see him clearly – the soft smile on his face, the closed eyes, his effortless concentration and serene acceptance. I felt secure, wrapped in the understanding which his meditation was unlocking. He had switched from speaking to meditating in a matter of seconds, and though there were no outward physical signs I sensed that the depth of his meditation was immense. I sat in silent awe.

The light in the room dimmed. Finally, Sangratan spoke:

'Tomorrow Shiv Saran will take into his body small quantities of gold, silver, lead and other minerals, as well as plants. He will do so for five days. They may ease his suffering and keep him alive. If he took them continuously or in huge doses they would surely hasten his death. I hope we will see the power of small actions.'

Sangratan lay down, covered himself with his shawl, and was soon fast asleep. I slept fitfully. A strange house, a hard sleeping surface, and the movement of the family members as they tended to Shiv Saran kept me from prolonged sleep. I lay and wondered what tomorrow would bring.

10

· ·

The Fourth Lesson of Life

It was a long night. I tossed and turned, conscious of the hardness of the mattress. Sangratan slept soundly. An hour before dawn he awoke. Immediately he was fully alert. 'Time to get up Bill-*ji*,' he said, raising himself and wrapping his cloak around him. Before I could stir he had left the room. I dragged my sleep-deprived body after him, slightly resentful of his fresh good humour, into the room where Shiv Saran lay, gaunt, frail, pale and in great pain. Sangratan placed a hand on his forehead. 'A low fever,' he said in a matter-of-fact tone. He placed his powerful arm under his patient and gently raised him to a sitting position. Shiv Saran groaned but said nothing. Sangratan took the cup with his most powerful medicine and held it to Shiv Saran's lips, speaking softly in the local dialect as Shiv Saran struggled to drink the mixture. Finally, all of it was consumed and Shiv Saran was gently laid back on his bed. Three more *rasais* (quilted blankets) were brought and placed on the *rasai* which was already covering him. Shiv Saran did not stir. He had turned on his side, his knees pulled up to his stomach. Consumed by pain, he did not seem to notice us as we crowded in the doorway.

Sujata sat cross-legged on the floor beside the low bed, her fragile hand on top of the coverings, generating love.

'There is nothing which needs to be done now,' said Sangratan, and then, turning to Sujata, he said, 'He will sleep and he will sweat. Try to keep him well covered for as long as possible.' She nodded and stared at Sangratan's face. Her own was full of the tough determination of one who has survived long years and many hardships. She would not give up her life partner without doing everything in her power to make him well. We all sensed that now was the time for Sujata and her husband to be alone so we retired in silence to the kitchen.

The kitchen was small with a sink at one end with green grimy shelving above it. Near the centre of the room stood a small wood-burning stove, with a round metal chimney rising up into the roof, another testament to this family's wealth. The soot-stained walls bore witness to the limited effectiveness of the chimney. The fire in the stove was lit, and we drank smoky water out of steel beakers. Sangratan explained that, in winter, when the snow would be four to six feet high and the temperature well below zero, the whole family would spend days on end in the warm closeness of this tiny room.

The sun came up, and cleared the peaks on the far side of the valley. After a breakfast of parathas, Sangratan and I looked in on Sujata and the ailing Shiv Saran. He lay as we had left him, and for a moment I thought he was dead. His face, only partly visible under the piles of bedding, was pale and still but the thin film of sweat on his forehead indicated that he was still alive. Sangratan again began a prolonged pulse-taking. Sujata watched in silence, scrutinising his face. Sangratan spoke to her and she silently left the room.

'This is not good, Bill-*ji*,' Sangratan said. 'Despite the power of the medicines our friend may not recover. I must stay here but you should not. Go back to your wife and child, for they need you. Kirti will take you, and I will see you tomorrow.' Sangratan's face had a thin smile. This was a kindly instruction, it was not a request.

I packed my bedding, collected my accoutrements and went

outside where Kirti was waiting and Sujata and her family were lined up to bid me farewell. Sangratan told me not to dally but to make good time in returning to Abha and Sean. We exchanged fond farewells and I was given little hugs by the children. Nandini gave me a jar of home-made pickle. After a short while, with a quick backward glance to ensure I was following, Kirti strode off down the track.

We made very good time. Kirti, foraging ahead, seemed to know the easiest way down the valley side, following waterways, finding small tracks, moving swiftly from clearing to clearing. Yesterday was all uphill, today all downhill. After a while my limbs loosened and, since the sun was still low in the sky, the air was pleasantly warm and walking a pleasure. We stopped regularly so that I could rest, and I warmed to this magnificent animal, my guide and protector in this beautiful wilderness.

We left the forest behind and passed isolated farms, always travelling downwards. We came to a well-used track, and soon the farmhouses were not so isolated. Apple and almond orchards and small vegetable plots lined our path, and increasing numbers of people could be seen working in the fields. We passed on and suddenly we came upon a metalled road. Kirti turned right, walked along the road a few yards, stopped and barked. She was telling me that this was the road to the farm where Abha and Sean were staying. It was time for her to return to Sangratan. I gave her a hug, and walked off down the road. She stood and watched long enough to decide that I knew what to do and then turned and disappeared back the way we had just come.

Another hour and I was entering the farmhouse. Abha was lying on the bed, shivering under a blanket, her face flushed with fever. 'You're back!' she said, surprise and relief on her face. She told me that she had had a fever when she awoke that morning and that Sean had gone with the local children to play on the hillside. I told her of my travels, and of Sujata and poor Shiv Saran, and of how Sangratan had told me to return to my family because, as he said, 'they need you.'

For the rest of the day I practised my loving kindness and compassion on Abha as she lay with a mild fever. Usually, I am not a good nurse, hoping that if the sick are left alone they will get better with the minimum of fuss. Today I consciously tried to anticipate Abha's every need. By evening her temperature had returned to normal and I had learnt that the joy in loving kindness and consideration is twofold: the joy which comes from freely giving care, attention and kindness, and the joy which comes from reciprocation. That night we slept warm and close.

The next morning I awoke as the sun rose above the peaks. I stepped outside and took deep breaths of fresh mountain air. Above me rose the Himalayas in all their glory, and before me nature at her most magnificent, green, lush, majestic and teeming. And in the pasture, about a hundred yards away, sat Kirti and Sangratan. I rushed down to meet them.

Sangratan asked after Abha and I told him she was well. I asked after Shiv Saran and he replied, 'He still lives.' I offered Sangratan food, but he said he had eaten, and the conversation drifted until finally he brought the conversation around to Shiv Saran again. He explained that, given the nature of existence, things will go wrong for us from time to time and suffering will occur despite our best efforts. He then told me the Fourth Lesson of Life.

The Fourth Lesson of Life shows us what to do when things go wrong. It helps us deal with the difficult problems that will confront us from time to time. It is particularly relevant to those times when obstacles block what we wish to do, or when things happen that we do not want to happen. In some ways it is the most important of all the Lessons of Life, for life is about dealing with problems.

The wise man knows what he values most, sees the obstacles to that which he seeks, and then either works round them, removes them, or accepts that he cannot have what he seeks and lives as best he can without it. The wise man also knows that pursuing what you cannot have is a waste of time and energy.

The Fourth Lesson of Life teaches us that when we find obstacles to what we seek, we must examine them to find out how to eliminate them. Knowing what we value and how much we value it is intrinsic to the Second Lesson of Life. The Third Lesson is to seek agreement in everything we do. The Fourth Lesson requires us to ask ourselves the following question when things do not go as we wish: What are the obstacles to us changing, nurturing or developing, and achieving that which brings us joy?

The question is simple. The answer requires concentrated meditation and mindfulness. For there are numerous answers to this question, depending on our circumstances. The obstacles can be within us, or within those around us. They can be the result of our actions past or present, or the actions of others; they can be the result of our living relationships; of the barrenness of the land; the type of climate; the nature of the wildlife, the plant life;

or any number of myriad phenomena. They can be different today than they were yesterday.

Often when we have a problem we look for someone to blame, or become emotional and worried. Our frustration leads us to ignore the obstacle. We become confused. However, if we concentrate on what we seek, and we meditate on the nature of the obstacle, our confusion disappears. We can see exactly both what it is we are seeking, and the obstacles to achieving it.

Once we can see what the obstacles are, we can work towards removing them, changing them, avoiding them or ignoring them. The removal of an obstacle removes the essence of the problem. Remembering the power of small actions, we must remove the obstacles one small step at a time.

The Fourth Lesson of Life also tells us that once we have identified the obstacles between a desired and an existing state, we must ask ourselves these questions:

*   How important for me is it that I change this situation?
*   Is the obstacle in the way of something I value highly?
*   Am I certain that I wish to deal with this or should I learn to live with it?

When we have answered these questions we know whether resolving the problem is something we greatly desire and is worthy of our efforts or if it is something we can easily live with. Knowing this we can decide whether or not to invest time and efforts in resolving the problem.

We must also remember that whatever we strive for, and whatever problems we resolve, new obstacles will always arise, and that in this constantly changing universe the 'perfect' object/

relationship/creature does not exist. To avoid suffering we should seek the ideal, but be prepared to accept circumstances which are as close to the ideal as we can get. Resolving our problems gets us closer to our ideal, but nothing is permanent.

Sometimes, no matter what we do, we are powerless even to approach our ideal situation. Sometimes our suffering is because someone who was with us is no longer with us and cannot return. We are bereaved. It is at times like these that our suffering is extreme, for it is living creatures with whom we find our greatest joy. Death is part of all our lives but it is an insurmountable obstacle. With bereavement, as with most things, there is no ideal resolution to the problem. The Lessons of Life teach us that we know the ideal but seek the best possible outcome. Since we cannot have the deceased in physical form, we must seek the next best thing. We must look for small things that will bring us as close to the ideal as possible. We must find what joy we can in the legacy of the deceased, in his or her greatest legacy, the children. We must find joy in our memories. To ease our suffering, each day we must seek some small way to nurture and develop those things that bring us nearer to the best we can achieve. This will not fill the gap left by the deceased, but it will ensure that the gap is filled as much as we can possibly fill it.

To summarise. The Fourth Lesson of Life teaches us that we must see clearly the obstacles to that which we seek to nurture and develop. We should concentrate on removing them one by one. When the obstacles are too great to remove, we minimise our suffering by acceptance of what is, and what can be.

11

The Fifth Lesson
of Life

As soon as he had finished recounting the Fourth Lesson of Life, Sangratan said his goodbyes and departed abruptly. His face wore a stern expression and the urgency of his pace as he traversed the track back to the ailing Shiv Saran had me concerned for the old man and his family. I stood and watched as he and Kirti disappeared from view. It was obvious that he felt something was amiss back at the farm, and that he was sorely needed.

The next morning he was back. Again he did not visit the farmhouse where we were staying, but was to be found a little way off, sitting with his faithful companion, waiting for me. I saw him by the track side as I ambled along on my morning walk. His smile was back, and Kirti came and brushed against me in greeting. I offered Sangratan some water from my water bottle but he refused.

'How is Shiv Saran?' I said.

'He is better, but he is not well. He will improve if you visit him and give him what is yours to give.' Sangratan looked away. He had been deliberately enigmatic, and I realised that he was seeking to find out how well I had learnt the Lessons of Life. 'I must get back,' he said, and rose and walked off along the track. I hurried after him and once more we were on our way back to the farm.

Shiv Saran was still in the bed, but the heavy covers had been replaced with a lightweight brown shawl. He lay still, gently snoring. He was gaunt, still drawn, but looked relaxed and at peace. He awoke as we entered and greeted us in heavily accented Hindi. Weak nods and gestures indicated he was better, but still very ill.

outside, Sangratan explained that the healing process had begun but, like all the cures of the Amchi, it would be a long time, perhaps a year or more, before Shiv Saran regained his vigour. All illness, he said, took a long time to develop, and the body took a long time to recover.

Seeing Shiv Saran lying there I had tried hard to think of what to give him. I understood that kindness and compassion were what Sangratan had alluded to when he said that I should 'give him what was mine to give', but I was perplexed as to what was the most appropriate way of expressing this kindness and compassion. I understood that by visiting and showing concern I was fulfilling the rudimentary kindness and compassion, but I wanted to exhibit as much kindness as possible for its own sake, and so that Sangratan would understand that I was learning well.

It was easy to express my concern for Shiv Saran for I genuinely admired him. Here was a man who had lived long years without the comforts and services that I had come to know and enjoy. His wiry frame was testimony to hard labour and a diet determined by what his hands could grow and what he could preserve through the long, cold snowed-in winter months. He was a man who, with his family beside him, had built the house we were in with his own hands; who, with guarded optimism, had survived the death of a beloved son; a man who had faced pain and illness with fortitude; who had dedicated his life to his family and to living a life of peace and harmony. It was easy to think of kind words for such a man, but difficult to think of what would bring him most joy.

I was moved by the sight of him, frail but tough, accepting

of his condition but stubbornly refusing to capitulate to it. I sat beside him on a home-made rug. His little granddaughter, Sangita, came in and sidled up to the bed, ignoring my presence. A tiny toddler hand reached out and stroked her grandfather's cheek. Her tiny fingers brushed his lips, and his old eyes lit up with pleasure and tenderness. 'Get better now,' the little girl said, in the language of the valley, as she gently stroked his face. Shiv Saran's eyes welled with tears, but the smile on his face was soft and warm. A few more strokes and Sangita decided she had done enough to make her grandfather better, and I suspect maybe she had. 'Small child and the power of small actions,' I thought to myself as she turned towards me, hands outstretched. By now she was convinced of the healing power of her hands. Grubby little fingers stroked my cheek as I, too, was given her healing touch.

It was over in seconds. She was distracted by the water bottle strung around my neck. Blue plastic was a rarity in these parts. I took it off, finally knowing how to express kindness and concern to the old man. As I placed it around the little girl's neck, her eyes widened and lit up with joy. Shiv Saran smiled at the look on his granddaughter's face, the source of his greatest joy.

I looked up to see everyone, including Sangratan, smiling at my actions. 'The presents we give are not restricted to the recipient, Bill-*ji*. A small act of kindness to one leads to joy for others, for we are all interdependent, and we find our greatest happiness in the happiness of others. You are learning well,' he said. I silently vowed to give more freely in future for I liked the feeling.

The rest of the day we spent enjoying the hospitality of

Sujata and her family. When afternoon turned to evening I took my leave of them all and, just before setting off, was given three bedraggled flowers collected by the delightful Sangita, a small bag of dried fruit from Sujata, a bottle of home-made spirits from Sanjay and Nandini. As quickly as I could I made my way back to my own family, thankful for my health and the company of kind-hearted people.

The next morning history repeated itself. Sangratan was back again, waiting by the side of the path, seeming to know my movements before I did. Time was running out for me as, soon, I would have to return to Delhi. I decided I needed to learn as much as possible from Sangratan so, for the next two days, I accompanied him while he walked the mountain trails from farm to farm. Sometimes someone had fallen ill, sometimes the person had an emotional problem and Sangratan would sit talking quietly while I enjoyed the hospitality of the home. Everywhere we went we were treated with kindness, concern and respect. Everywhere we were offered precious food and delicacies. I thought it was because I was with him that we were received so hospitably, but Sangratan explained that they were like this with all visitors for they had learnt the Fifth Lesson of Life, a lesson about respect and giving, designed to promote harmonious living.

During our travels Sangratan would comment on what makes for harmonious living. On the evening of the fourth day he clarified the origins and explained the content of the Fifth Lesson of Life. This is what he told me:

Whereas the first four Lessons of Life are drawn from diverse ancient texts, it is said that the Fifth Lesson of Life was the work of one man. This Lesson was produced in an attempt to unify the strands of the previous four. It is not certain who compiled the Fifth Lesson. Some say it was Tenzin himself, but this cannot be. Whoever it was, it was an obvious attempt to codify kind and compassionate behaviour, and give guidance on how to treat others.

Over the centuries, as change occurred, even the true Amchi have put aside the original list of actions which comprised the Fifth Lesson. The utility of the original list was always in question, for, unlike the other Lessons of Life which give general guidelines on living, the Fifth Lesson was comprised of a list of specified actions, and it was far too prescriptive. The original Lesson laid down which jar of *archar** was to be taken when visiting a relative, what type of present should be given to a stranger, and what kind words were to be given in welcome. The original Fifth Lesson was far too dogmatic and the true Amchi rejects dogma. What remains with the true Amchi today, and what we remind our people of from time to time, are the principles of living on which the original Fifth Lesson of Life is based.

Much of what was written in the Fifth Lesson of Life you see all around you here in these valleys, and it would seem that whoever compiled it simply took existing practices and incorporated them into a list of dos and don'ts. What I and all

---

* Spicy pickle

true Amchi teach today is not this code but the general principles underlying it.

The Fifth Lesson teaches us that we should be mindful of the wondrous nature of our existence, how we are the result of a long chain of life which stretches back further than we can imagine, over millions and millions of years. It reminds us that we owe what form and consciousness we have now to eons of change, struggle, suffering and re-formation. We owe our existence as it is today not only to every living thing that has gone before us but also to everything around us in the present moment, since we are interdependent.

The Fifth Lesson teaches us that we must be mindful that everything that exists now, including ourselves, will become everything that will exist in the future. We create the future of all living things as we shape ourselves and our world, and by our responses as the world shapes us. We must therefore be mindful of our infinite past and infinite future. The Fifth Lesson requires us to be aware of the consequences of the smallest of our actions and to live a life of openness, respect and generosity.

The Fifth Lesson stresses that we should develop five personal qualities to help us in our dealings with others. The first of these qualities is closely related to the First Lesson of Life, which teaches us to examine what it is we value. The Fifth Lesson tells us that we should develop *self-knowledge* through meditation and by being mindful of the world, and our own natures.

The second quality we need to develop is also related to the First Lesson of Life. As we examine and re-examine our values, we should develop an *understanding of our true value as sentient creatures*. By doing so we understand our own worth and enhance our self-respect.

The third quality we need to develop helps us when we are seeking agreement. It is *respect for others*, not only their similarities to but their differences from us, even those differences we do not find acceptable. For instance, while we do not eat the flesh of other sentient creatures, we still respect those who do. By respecting and showing kindness to those with whom we have differences, we enhance the possibility of them learning from our example and changing. This respect for others requires that we pay them attention, listen carefully to them and understand their feelings and their needs.

The fourth quality that we should develop is *conscious giving*. We should give our time, our attention and our kindness and compassion freely and on every occasion when we meet with another. In these mountains in ancient times a code of behaviour for dealing with each other, and with guests, was based on the ability to give. Even today, when local people have forgotten the origins of their traditions, you can still see this quality in the way they treat each other. The ability to give is found everywhere in these mountains, for they know the joy that giving brings: no one comes away from a farmhouse without having received something. And when the inhabitants of these farmhouses visit they take a gift. It may be small – some dried fruit, a jar of pickles – but it is not a token, it is a gift of great value for the giver has considered the need of the recipient and chosen it with care to maximise the joy of the receiver. The Fifth Lesson of Life tells us that the value of what is given is enhanced by the giving.

Food given with love and kindness is enhanced by love and kindness. Food kept for ourselves is only a means of fuelling the body. If we are to have joy in our lives, we must find the enhanced value in giving.

The Fifth Lesson of Life which the Amchi teach today stresses that in all our dealings with other sentient beings, we must cultivate principles of respect and generosity. The practice of conscious giving is kindness and compassion made real, and kindness and compassion creates harmony. Conscious giving means that we must consciously give our time, energy, words and material goods to those we meet, each time we meet.

The Fifth Lesson of Life also tells us that we must seek to understand, to give respect, and develop our capacity to give with *openness* and clarity, not to impose our will on others, but so that others can know what we honestly need and freely give to us.

In these mountains there are not many who cannot express their needs and feelings, for this openness is highly valued by all. If we are sad we cry, we wail, we beat our chests, we express our anguish. If we are happy we laugh, we shout, we dance. There are no stiff upper-lips here! We are open about out lack of knowledge. If we want to know, we ask, we do not hide behind the manners of some town-dwellers.

The Fifth Lesson tells us that if we do not have 'openness' we are being disrespectful. We do not say things are fine when they are not, or 'yes' when we mean 'no'. We do not hide how we feel. We say openly, but with kindness, all that is important for us to say. We love to express ourselves so that we can know ourselves better, and people can know us; honestly and sincerely. The Fifth

Lesson reminds us that if we close off our feelings and our thoughts, barriers of ignorance will be constructed between us and others and they will not know what it is we need or be able to give it with kindness. Also, if we are not open we cannot expect others to be open with us; we make and reinforce a way of behaving which makes kindness harder to give.

Not saying what we feel, or what we want to happen, or what we want to know is disrespectful to others. It causes others to work harder to understand what we really want, or how we really feel. It is an obstacle to kindness and an obstacle to harmony. The Fifth Lesson states that we must overcome the selfishness of shyness, and be open with others.

The development of self-knowledge, understanding of our true value as sentient creatures, respect for others, conscious giving and openness requires meditation and mindfulness. We must meditate on who or what we are, our origins, our relationship with others, our needs in relation to others and theirs to us. We must be mindful each time we meet with another that we find something to give which will enhance their joy. It can be a word, a warm embrace, a small gift or service. Whatever it is, 'conscious giving' brings joy, for conscious giving is the essence of kindness, and kindness creates harmony. If we practise 'openness' we remove barriers to ignorance and help create greater understanding, and understanding reduces suffering. The Fifth Lesson of Life requires us to nurture self-knowledge, understanding of our value as sentient creatures, respect for others, conscious giving and openness so that we can practise loving kindness and compassion.

12

....

Fearful Prophecies

It was my last night in Kinnuer. Again the day had been cold and overcast. I looked for Sangratan in the morning but he was nowhere to be seen. In the afternoon I drove to Peo for provisions for the journey back to Delhi and on the way back I saw him sitting in a clearing on the edge of the forest. Waiting. I greeted him warmly, relieved to see him one last time, and he told me that he too was leaving in the morning, travelling north-east along the old Hindustan Tibet road towards China. We would be travelling in opposite directions.

He said he was staying that night in a farmhouse a little way off, and that he had come to the road hoping to see me before we both left. He laughed heartily when I told him he seemed to have mystical powers.

'How else would you know where to find me?' I said, and he laughed again.

'Your car was not at the farmhouse and this is the only road this side of the valley. I knew you had to drive back this way,' he said with a chuckle.

'You knew my name before we met,' I said with a slight hint of exasperation at the mirth my comments elicited. 'That day at Tulsi's when you greeted me by name, when we had never set eyes on each other before.'

Sangratan suppressed another bout of laughter. 'Have you never thought that almost all of the people around here might know the name of the *gori pharungi** who chooses to come and stay

---

* Literal translation: 'white foreigner'.

in a farmhouse in this valley?' he said. 'Maybe I was told by one of them?' He put an arm around my shoulder. 'All mysteries in life can usually be explained through rational means, though some have stranger explanations than we can know at this stage of our existence.'

I was comforted by his reassuring arm and his kindly tone, and my exasperation dissipated in the chilly evening air. Sangratan wrapped his shawl around him and I took a blanket from the car. On the edge of the forest as the day grew dark we lit a fire and in the firelight we sat and talked for what was to be the last time. Sangratan had many questions for me. I told him of my life, of the things I valued greatly. The words that I spoke came from deep inside me, and I saw my life with a clarity that I had never known before. I told him of my relationships, past and present, the people I had loved and those I loved now. I told him what gave me joy and of my resolve to change, to pursue a more harmonious, joyful existence; of my determination to spend more time with my son and savour his childhood as I had savoured mine with my father. I told him of my past foolishness in the single-minded pursuit of career and material wealth which had created an imbalance in my existence to the detriment of my family and the other things I valued. I told him I would nurture the joy that 'conscious giving' brings. Sangratan listened and I poured out my heart to him, and felt totally accepted for who I really was. When I had finished, he was silent, and I realised he was giving me time to collect my thoughts and decide if there was anything else I wanted to say. There was not. I sat and watched the flames in the tiny fire, and as the last of the daylight faded away I felt at peace with myself.

We sat in silence for a long while, then Sangratan reached out and placed the last of the dead wood on the fire.

'Tell me about the world outside these mountains,' he said. 'I have heard dreadful tales of the behaviour of men towards nature and other sentient creatures.'

I told him of our world, of nations' capacity to build and destroy. I told him of the worldwide pollution, and of the great wealth of some and the poverty of others, and of the huge socially constructed differences between the rich and the poor. I told him the little I knew about new technologies, of computers and satellites, of space travel and how man was planning to go to Mars. Sangratan listened quietly, prompting periodically, obviously uneasy. He told me how life was changing even here in the forests and the valleys. He spoke of the waste and corruption, and the destruction of trees that had lived and thrived for three hundred years. 'Follow the road which runs by the river and you will find many scars that men are inflicting,' he said.

I told him that this was paradise compared with much of the rest of the world and explained about the disappearance of the world's forests. At last he said with a finality, 'It is that time already!' And he fell silent. He was smiling his gentle smile but tears had formed in his eyes. The fire died and night closed in around us. It was time for me to leave. I promised to return to the same spot in the morning to say goodbye. With a silent nod he turned and walked into the forest. I drove slowly back to the farmhouse.

That night the bed seemed too hard and the room too cold. I lay awake, thinking of the way we live and of Sangratan's words. At around 4 a.m. I got up and looked out on the quiet, beautiful, moonlit valley, and waited for the dawn. At first light I drove to where I had left Sangratan. As I got out of the car I could see he had his meagre belongings packed and was ready for his long walk. From his countenance I realised he was still troubled, but he greeted me warmly. He told me that we now must part and, placing both hands on my shoulders, he looked into my eyes and said, 'All the signs indicate that terrible times lie ahead. Many problems will face mankind. A time is coming when the earth will undergo many small changes to engender a new balance. These changes are the culmination of millions and millions of mindless small changes wrought by men. The signs are everywhere to be seen that change is coming to the world we know. If we open our eyes we can see these changes coming.'

We sat and for the last time we were student and teacher. This is his last teaching:

The Lessons of Life tell us that we, as men and women, exist in harmony as long as we consciously nurture and develop the world to sustain us. The Lessons of Life came into being to help us to avoid conflict and live in harmony, but they have been forgotten and ignored. When the Lessons were being compiled it was predicted that unless men learnt practical ways of living in harmony with nature there would come a day when the elements would rebel and reassert the equilibrium that men and women in their thoughtlessness threatened to destroy. It was stated that when we do not consciously nurture and develop and simply use and exploit and discard, then that which we are dependent upon suffers and, with that suffering, our own suffering increases.

We have known for centuries that we are dependent on all phenomena, as all phenomena are dependent on us, and we know that it is all phenomena that we must consciously nurture and develop. To do this we must examine and understand the rhythm of life and change. We must know ourselves and what we need to sustain us, and how to sustain that which sustains us. The Lessons of Life were compiled in the belief that men and women want to live in peace and harmony and it is only thoughtlessness which prevents them from doing so.

The Lessons of Life came into existence centuries ago because harmony and balance were lacking in these mountains. How much worse the situation in these mountains and the whole world is now! Millions upon millions of men and women disregard thoughts of harmony and practise their deluded selfishness. Where sustenance is ignored in favour of competition and gross consumption. Millions are engaged in competition with each other for the possession of the materials and the creatures of the earth. They abdicate responsibility for their lives, their being and their world in the competition to consume, increasing the suffering of the world and themselves in a thoughtless competition which confronts the natural balance.

As men and women move further away from nature and the natural world into a world increasingly designed and constructed of man-made materials, they lose sight of the natural world and the natural order. It is almost inevitable that, without a conscious effort, they do not think of nature and their natural relationship to the world. Everything which is placed before them has been designed and fashioned, constructed and altered, so that it bears little resemblance to its original naturalness. Once they lose sight of nature, their thoughts are shaped by the synthetic world in which they live and they increasingly think less of the natural world and the natural balance.

They eat flesh with little thought for the animal. They use dead trees with little thought for the forests. They eat bread with little thought for the fields, rain or the sun, or the labour of the farmer. They wear fabric with little thought for the plants or the animal from which it comes. They produce and consume with only the minimum of thought of what it actually is they are consuming, or the destruction involved in producing. They view dead flesh, muscle and fat, and see only food. They look at a chair and see only a piece of furniture.

In their increasingly designed, fashioned, altered and constructed state, they do not see the hands that make, or the hands that harvest, reap and sow. They become estranged from the natural world, and their thoughts are less of nature and increasingly of their man-made environment.

This tendency to become thoughtless about the wonder of things has always been with us. The Buddha, when teaching mindfulness to children, shared with them a tangerine. He told them to eat it and be mindful of what they were doing. He explained that with mindfulness we experience the lovely fragrance and sweet taste, and so much more. We are aware of the texture and the beautiful colour. With mindfulness we can see the tangerine tree, the tangerine blossom in spring, the soil from which it draws its nutrients, the sun and rain which nourish it, as well as the labour and care of the farmer. With complete mindfulness we can see the wonder of life and the relationship of all things in a single object.

Today men and women live without mindfulness, and the world suffers. They see what is in front of them but are not mindful of what truly is, or how it came to be. They are without awareness. The Buddha also explained what it was like to *eat* a tangerine without awareness. For example, when we peel the tangerine with mindfulness we experience the texture and softness. When we put a slice in our mouth we experience all the sensations that eating a tangerine gives. Those who eat without awareness, feel only the surface of the tangerine. When they smell the fragrance they do not know what they are smelling. They do not know the wondrous nature of the tangerine and they are not aware of what they are eating! Without mindfulness the tangerine is not real to them, it is only something to consume.

I have been to towns and seen how town-dwellers separate themselves from that which sustains them. They put concrete between them and the earth. They put cars and other machines between them and travelling. They put distance between themselves and all objects. They do not see the forest grow, or the trees chopped down, or the wooden objects made, they do not see the men and women labour in the fields, the crops grow, the animals slaughtered, the millions of tiny organisms which create the fields. They see only the object of their purchase. Many do not see the sunrise or the day grow dark. They spend their lives in unnatural rhythms, in unnatural light, separated from life and nature. They do not see the natural world so they do not nurture and develop it. Soon the consequences of this estrangement will be upon us all.

We are nearing the time which has been predicted, a time when the very balance of the world as we know it will be overturned and, as a result, great catastrophes will befall mankind. Already whole species have disappeared, their billions of years of contribution to the development of the world obliterated.

The signs are obvious, we are living in a world where, because of man's actions, the very balance of the elements is being usurped. I have seen the signs and wanted not to recognise them, for even here we will know some of the suffering which will befall all of Bharat* and the lands to the north. Here in the next few years great floods will fill some of these valleys and the changes in the winds will affect the lands which surround these mountains, and they too will suffer as never before. The very soil will rebel at its plundering and contamination.

It has been predicted by the ancients that at the time when the elements seek a new equilibrium, some rivers will cease to flow while others will burst their banks and inundate the land. Some crops will fail through excessive heat and drought, while others will perish through flood and deluge. Millions of homes will be swept away and dis-ease, which always accompanies change in water levels, will take the lives of many.

People also will change, for the smallest changes in the elements affect us, as the smallest of changes in us affect the elements. Sadly, history bears repeated witness that when

---

* India.

thoughtless men are faced with new situations they resort to confrontation and violence. Man will fight man because of a shortage of precious water, and thousands will perish. Violence is what those who do not seek harmony always resort to when deluded selfishness brings hardship. All this will happen here in Bharat.

When I was young I saw the suffering that self-deluded man visited on others when imbalance occurred and famine came. In the coming days when shortages occur through the mindless action of millions, those same millions will ensure further suffering. In the time of shortage, men will kill others in huge numbers over 'their' land, 'their' homes, 'their' scarce resources, 'their' water. It is a logical progression of thoughtlessness, and it will happen. It will happen here and in the lands around.

Do not think there is a mystery in these predictions, for there is none. If we do not nurture and develop, balance and harmonise, then the changes which occur will bring us suffering. When we practise selfishness and possessiveness in our personal relationships we cause suffering to ourselves and those around us. When we practise selfishness and possessiveness with all of the natural world we cause suffering to all humanity. The signs show that the world is sorely suffering and all need to learn the Lessons of Life, and begin to develop and nurture mindfulness and compassion which are the pillars on which harmony is built.

Suffering in the world, like illness within the body, takes time to manifest itself in a chronic condition and, like an illness within the body, suffering outside of it also takes a long time to heal. It is only small, sustained, everyday selfless actions by men and women which will restore harmony and ease the suffering which now will surely come. Dark days are coming. Everywhere we will need to learn and practise the Lessons of Life if we are to prosper and thrive.

Sangratan finished his discourse. It was time for both of us to leave: he to walk the mountain path, and I to travel by car on the metalled road. I thought about how he would experience each small step, the mountains, the flowers, the pasture, the rivers and the streams; while I would career along not daring to take my eyes off the road in front of me for fear of hurtling into the abyss, and the raging torrent that is the Sutlej river. I thought of Sangratan's amusement when I first used the word 'career' to him, and our respective journeys seemed an apt metaphor for our different ways of life. For a moment I was overcome with a deep sadness, for it seemed both were doomed.

Sangratan read my thoughts. 'I am old,' he said. 'The travelling Amchi's days are numbered, but I will walk out my days. Hospitals are coming to the valleys. It is a change which I both regret and welcome: for the need and usefulness of a hospital is great. Let us hope that the hospitals and the healing are made with mindfulness, and by those who have learnt the Lessons of Life.'

My face must have betrayed my feelings, for he continued: 'Do not be sad. Your life is yours. You can live it with awareness, pursuing the things you value, seeking agreements with kindness, compassion and respect, and with conscious giving and openness.

You can live in harmony with the things you value if you follow the Lessons of Life. And if you follow them your small actions will make the world a better place for others. Remember, this life is short, but the effects of our actions linger on with our children, and our friends, and all the other sentient beings we nurture and develop. Small actions today have mighty consequences, and life is made up of small actions.' He embraced me again and my spirits were lifted. 'We will meet again, Bill-*ji*, but for now we must part. Peace be with you.'

I stood and watched as he turned and walked off along the forest path, one of the last of the travelling Amchi, striding out through the tree-lined valley as the Amchi have done for hundreds of years. When I could no longer see him I got into the car and made my way back to the farmhouse to begin the journey home.

Epilogue

The journey was arduous. An eleven-hour drive to Shimla, and another nine hours to Delhi. The road from Kalpa to Shimla was narrow, twisting, uneven and prone to landslides. Abha and I took turns at the wheel. Neither of us had wanted to leave the clean air, the sparkling streams, the beautiful mountains and gentle people. We drove in silence, as fast as we dared on the treacherous mountain road, each determined to return as soon and as often as possible to this beautiful, isolated area.

Back in Delhi we changed our lives. Using the Five Lessons as my guide, I gradually rearranged my life so that I could pursue those things that gave me the greatest joy, and so that I could spend more time with the people I most admired and loved. I gave up thoughts of career to pursue those things and relationships I valued most.

I made sure that I was home when Sean returned from school, and that each day we would have lunch together. In the process I found the joy my father must have found in my company when I was a child, and I began to understand him and myself a little better. The lunches with Sean turned into longer afternoon sessions, for he began to sit with me in my office doing his homework, while I sat working on whatever project was at hand. My father used to tell me that he was the best friend I would ever have, and that he was worried that he loved me too much. Now I know exactly what he meant, for I realise just how much he loved me.

Before meeting Sangratan and learning the Lessons of Life

I was estranged from my eldest son, Ben, a young man of twenty-one who was not following in his father's footsteps. I saw only the minor differences between us; I did not see his admirable qualities. The Lessons of Life helped me to see him as he is, and taught me not to impose my will on him. With small steps our relationship has improved, and we too are now beginning to share again the closeness we had when he was a child.

Once I began to practise what the Lessons of Life teach, my life changed in so many other ways. I realised that there were many things that I had enjoyed when I was young which I had put aside in pursuit of a career. I used to love to swim but I had not been swimming for years. I used to be soccer mad, playing and coaching, but circumstances had conspired to stop that activity. I love music, both listening and playing, but my guitar had been put aside and I could never find the time to listen to tapes or CDs. I rediscovered so many things which I loved to do which I had put aside, for the sake of a career, or because situations changed, or because it seemed that I was too old to pursue them. I also discovered lots of situations I wished to change, new things that I wished to pursue, and new people I wished to meet. The Lessons of Life helped clarify and organise my life, and changed the way I interacted with people on a day to day basis.

I started to swim every night and rediscovered the pleasure I used to have in that activity, and also the joy that regular exercise brings. Once I got a little fitter I took up coaching soccer again and found the joy of helping little children and the pleasure of group activities. I rediscovered the joy of playing and listening to music and found many new friends with the same interests. And that's not all. Through a new musical friend I discovered the joy of performing and entertaining others. At fifty years of age I wrote and performed a comedy show at a packed theatre in Delhi. It was the first time since a school production at the age of ten that I had been on stage! My confidence to try new things grew, and I took up gardening and woodwork, to be closer to nature and the process of physical production. Even though I am not an expert in these activities, I learnt new things about wood, about plants, about growth and the ever-changing rhythms of life. By practising the self-examination that the Lessons of Life require, I continue to learn new things about myself, about how I grow and change too. My life has become far more fulfilling and satisfying. My relationships have deepened and new ones have blossomed.

Most importantly I realised that the pursuit of money and excessive material goods dominated my life. I lived like a Raja but was always pursuing more. I had taken on clients because they were willing to pay large sums of money. I gave little thought to the values of the enterprise I was helping, or price I was paying in terms of time with my family and conflict with my values. All of this changed. Through the Lessons of Life I stopped pursuing money, and sought out the company of good people. I began to evaluate all my actions against my examined values. Life became so much richer.

In the summers, when the passes re-opened, Abha, Sean and I with some close friends would return to Kinnuer, but Sangratan the Amchi was never there. I have searched for him throughout the whole of the region to no avail. No one had seen him. Yet I have seen the changes coming to Kinnuer. The government has been successfully promoting agriculture and the tribal people are being encouraged to grow apples as a cash crop. The forests are being chopped down as orchards expand, and with their new-found cash wealth the apple-growing farmers are seeking wood to build new, palatial farmhouses. In Kalpa a hospital has been built. It is big, empty and planned and constructed without the mindfulness required to meet the needs of the people. The road to Kinnuer is being widened to accommodate the apple lorries, and it is opening the region to other visitors for whom no proper infrastructure has been provided. Each year a few more tourists visit the region and more and more TV satellite dishes are to be seen.

In the summer of 1997 the Sutlej overflowed and swept away a vital road bridge. Floods ravaged the valley, breaking down the mountain side and creating a temporary lake one and a quarter kilometres long, cutting off Kinnuer from Simla. Sangratan's prophecies were beginning to be fulfilled. That summer I did not go to Kinnuer. I spent my holiday in rainy, constructed England, daydreaming of Kinnuer.

I returned to India in July, back to the heat and humidity of a Delhi summer. Time passed, and I had almost given up hope of meeting Sangratan again when one evening in the late summer my doorbell rang. At my door was a young Sikh man. He said that his name was Ranjit, and that he had just returned from Kinnuer. He told me that on the last day of his camping holiday he saw an old man sitting by the side of the road. As he passed, the old man called Ranjit by his name. 'Good morning, Ranjit-*ji*, I had hoped we would meet,' the old man said. When Ranjit asked him how he knew his name, the old man replied with a broad smile, 'There is no mystery, we know many things here.' Was the old man accompanied by a big black dog? The answer was yes. Was it Sangratan the Amchi? Of course it was!

Sangratan asked Ranjit if he would be travelling to Delhi and the young man said that he did not live in Delhi, but he would be travelling there. He asked Ranjit to give me a message, but Ranjit protested that he did not know me, and that Delhi was a big place. Sangratan told Ranjit that the world was not as big a place as he imagined, and with a sweet smile insisted that Ranjit would know of me, and that he would learn of my address.

Their conversation, though brief, was unnerving for young Ranjit, who told me that Sangratan was most serene and most convincing. He continued to assure Ranjit that he would learn my address, and that he and I would meet. It was only after they had parted that Ranjit's scepticism reasserted itself; only afterwards did he feel a little foolish in believing this old man of the mountains.

By the time Ranjit got to Delhi he had dismissed the conversation with Sangratan and thought no more of it. However, on his first full day in Delhi he came across a piece of paper, part of a marketing letter I had distributed, with my name, address and telephone number on! That he should find my details was such an incredible coincidence that, instead of simply phoning, Ranjit decided to call round to my house in person.

On a sticky Delhi evening, Ranjit stood at my door and I invited him in. We drank lime sodas and he conveyed to me Sangratan's greetings. He told me that Sangratan was fit and well and full of joy. He also said he did not understand Sangratan's message to me but that Sangratan had said I would know what it meant. He repeated the message as Sangratan had spoken it. Sangratan had told him to tell me to share the Lessons of Life. Ranjit described how Sangratan promised that he and I would meet again before the end of the millennium, and that on a certain date I should visit a place in Himachal Pradesh and wait for him there.

On that day I will be waiting for him or, more likely, he will be waiting for me. I will tell him how he has changed my life, how the Lessons of Life have helped me find myself, and of all the powerful small changes which have helped me find fulfilment. I will tell him of this book, how this is my way of sharing the Lessons of Life, the teachings of Sangratan the Amchi.

Appendices

APPENDIX I

THE FIVE LESSONS OF LIFE AND HOW TO APPLY THEM

THE FIRST LESSON OF LIFE

In the First Lesson of Life (see Chapter 3), Sangratan explains that to live in harmony with yourself you must examine and periodically re-examine what you value, and decide how important it is to you. When you know this you have the beginnings of a blueprint for action.

Determining Your Values

1. Think of the things and people you value most. Give yourself plenty of time to do this, in an environment where you will not be disturbed.
2. On a piece of paper, list all those things that you value most, and why you value them. Include such things as family relationships, health, career, religion, hobbies.
3. Try to number them in order of importance, beginning at 1.
4. Examine your choices. Be honest with yourself. Consider the questions below and, if you find it helpful, jot down your answers.
    * What do you spend most of your free time thinking about, or wishing for?
    * What have you always wanted?
    * What gives you most pleasure?

* What ways of behaving do you find most admirable?
* Are there things you enjoyed as a child which you were told to put away for the sake of a career or a relationship? If so, do you still value them?
* Whom do you admire most and why?
* What attributes do you most value?

5. When you have considered these questions, look again at the list of things you value. Is there a contradiction between your most important values and what you spend most of your life wishing, craving, wanting or working for?

6. If there seems to be a contradiction, look again at what you have written. If necessary, rearrange your list to ensure it reflects the true importance of the things you value.

Remember

For those who want to live in harmony with themselves, this process of assessment is the first step, for it is the things that you value that give purpose to your life. However, this assessment should not be seen as a once-in-a-lifetime process. Whenever you review your life, you should also review your underlying values, for as you gain experience and years, and as things change around you, the importance of many of the things you value changes.

THE SECOND LESSON OF LIFE

In the Second Lesson of Life (see Chapter 4) Sangratan shows you how to begin to arrange your life so that what is important to you is what you pursue most vigorously. You learn how to work towards steadily improving your life in the areas that matter the most to you. You learn that the nurturing and development of what you value is an ongoing, everyday activity.

In order to nurture and develop those things you value, you must also remember the following:

1. Because everything changes, that which we value must be nurtured and developed every day.

2. Everything has its time. Appreciate the power of small actions. Keep your destination in mind and by small actions work towards it.

3. At the beginning of the day, answer these questions:
    *   Today, how can I enhance and develop that which I most value?
    *   Today, how can I fill my life with that which I most value?
    *   Today I intend to improve my relationships by —
    *   Today I intend to make the following small adjustments/changes —

4. At the end of the day, answer these questions:
    *   What have I done today to enhance that which I most value?
    *   What have I done today to develop that which I most value?
    *   Today I discovered that I —
    *   I was disappointed/happy that —

THE THIRD LESSON OF LIFE

In the Third Lesson of Life (see Chapter 6) Sangratan explains that to live in harmony and effectively pursue what you value, you need to see that the differences between humans and all other sentient beings are very small. You also need to seek agreement for your plans and actions with others wherever possible, particularly with those to whom you give the greatest value. He tells you to meditate, seek agreement, then act to nurture and develop what you most value.

I.   To see the similarities between yourself and the one with whom you are in conflict, you must focus on yourself and the situation and not on the antagonist. Focus on how *you* can resolve the situation, for it is your actions you can control best. In the following exercise, the objective is to focus on you and the other person as human beings in the same situation. Answer the following questions honestly:

* Why do I value ... [add name]?
* I appreciated it when he/she —
* I resented it when he/she —
* He/she resented it when I —
* He/she appreciated it when I —
* How can I improve the situation?

Remember

Those who want to live in harmony with others must see the similarities, not just the differences. This makes it easier to tolerate differences in a new way. By nurturing similarities and tolerating differences you will find it easier to reach agreement, to create harmony, and to pursue what you most value.

2.   Appreciate the benefits that agreement brings:

* Agreement will minimise future conflict and maximise harmony.
* Agreement promotes understanding and openness.
* Agreement will increase your productive capacity.

3. By seeking areas of agreement for your plans and actions you:
    * Clarify to yourself and others what we intend to do.
    * You involve all in the decision-making process.
    * You give others the opportunity to state their needs.
    * You give yourself the opportunity to hear alternative views.
    * You give yourself the opportunity to gain assistance and the involvement of others in your projects.
    * You strengthen your resolve to change by making your declaration of intent.

THE FOURTH LESSON OF LIFE

In the Fourth Lesson of Life (see Chapter 10), Sangratan shows you what to do when things go wrong. It helps you to deal with difficult problems and shows you how to approach problems at work or at home so that they can be resolved in the most effective way possible. Because of constant change you need constantly to adjust. From time to time it is necessary to find new ways of dealing with the problems that change presents.

1. When things do not go as you wish, consider giving precise and detailed answers to the following questions:
    * What desired state am I seeking?
    * What are the obstacles to me changing, nurturing or developing, and achieving that which brings me joy?

2.   Do not seek only one general answer, but several specific answers which can be used as the basis for small, day-to-day changes. For example: imagine you are in a relationship with a close relative which is causing you to suffer. There is animosity and behaviour which hurts you. Ask yourself:

   *   What is the ideal desired state that I wish to obtain? Answer: *Ideally*, I seek to live in complete harmony with my relative.

   *   What is an acceptable desired state that I can realistically achieve? Answer: *Realistically*, I seek an end to hostile behaviour; to gain an appropriate level of trust; and that he/she does not speak ill of me in future.

3.   Next consider what *exactly* you mean by the above answers. It may be that you want him/her to refrain from making disparaging remarks about, say, your weight. Or for him/her to stop scoffing at your attempts to cook. Or for him/her to stop telling your friends about an embarrassing incident.

4.   What are the obstacles to achieving these specific small changes? List them. By examining each obstacle you give yourself a framework for seeking a resolution to the problem facing you. The answers people give to this question usually revolve round the other person's behaviour, but Sangratan teaches that it is *your* responsibility to pursue agreement, irrespective of the other person's beliefs. You must accept your relative's hurtful behaviour and concentrate on ways to promote agreement. For example:

the following obstacles *can* be addressed:

*   You may not have told the relative calmly and with kindness how you feel about his/her remarks, and that you want him/her to stop.

*   You may not have shown him/her loving kindness and compassion because you remember his/her past behaviour.

*   It might be that you simply do not understand why he/she behaves in this way and therefore do not know where to start to change the situation.

    In all of the above situations (and there can be many more), the onus is on *you* to put right what you see as a problem.

5. Once you have examined and identified each obstacle, you can draw up a plan to eliminate them. Each day you need to do something to remove at least one of the obstacles to your desired state.

6. The Fourth Lesson of Life reminds you that, sometimes, despite your best efforts, the obstacles to your desired state remain. If you cannot remove the obstacles you must accept the situation. So, if your relative still behaves hurtfully towards you after you have done all in your power to create harmony, at least you have the satisfaction of knowing that you have done everything you could to make matters better. This in itself is some comfort and can be a springboard to drawing up another strategy. For example: Since you cannot find harmony when you meet, you might work towards avoiding your abusive relative.

THE FIFTH LESSON OF LIFE

In the Fifth Lesson of Life (see Chapter 11), Sangratan teaches you how to behave with other people. To live harmoniously, you need to develop five attributes through meditation and mindfulness. These are:

* Self-knowledge
* Understanding your true value as a sentient creature
* Respect for others
* Conscious giving
* Openness

1. Self-knowledge is achieved through meditation and by examining how you feel about the various situations you face, and what you would like to happen. It is important to examine and re-examine your reactions and feelings and not take them for granted. You can work towards finding a blueprint for future action by asking yourself the following questions for each situation you face:

   * What went on here?
   * Why did I behave the way I did?
   * How do I feel about what went on?
   * How do I feel about my reactions?
   * What would I have liked to have happened?
   * How would I like to have reacted?

2. Understanding your true value as a sentient creature. To do this we should meditate on the nature of all living things, and their relationship and similarities with ourselves. In chapter twelve, Sangratan tells us that the Buddha uses the example of eating a tangerine with mindfulness when teaching young

children. We should practice Buddhist 'Mindful Consciousness' in all our dealings with living things.

3.   Respect for others requires you to understand their feelings and needs. To do this you must listen carefully to what they say. By asking others what they want and listening to their replies you are better able to give them the kindness and compassion they need (and not what you think they need!) In the smallest of your interactions you shape the whole of the present and the future. This fact makes it imperative that you give the utmost respect to all other living things.

4.   Conscious giving. Each time you meet another person you should give them something; it can be a kind word, a gesture, a smile, gift or service. You should consciously cultivate *giving* as a part of every interaction. Meditate on how you can give to others and reflect after every meeting on whether you gave a kind word, or acted kindly, or gave something to increase the joy of others. Remember that, by offering small daily acts of generosity, you make the world a better place.

5.   Openness. The cultivation of openness is also important. It is wise to seek open relationships in which you can tell others what you would like to happen, and others can tell you what they would like to happen. When openness is practised along with loving kindness and compassion, harmony is increased and suffering diminished. Openness requires that you:

　*　 Tell people what you want to happen instead of always doing what you think they want you to do.

* Express your feelings.
* Let people know what you think of them, so that they know how to respond to you.
* Overcome your shyness. (To do this you should follow the Fourth Lesson of Life and seek to change your behaviour through small steps.)

APPENDIX II

MEDITATING ON SUFFERING

When explaining the ways of the Amchi, Sangratan says that ideas and beliefs do and should change through time and circumstance. You should not cling to beliefs when their utility has ceased. He explains that all beliefs are an amalgam and that belief systems are ever-changing and interdependent.

In Chapter 9 we saw Sangratan tell Sujata to meditate on death. Through rational meditation it becomes possible to understand things better, and with understanding suffering is alleviated. Rational meditation can be used by anyone to help deal with any phenomenon, situation, object or person.

1. For any meditation to be effective you must be undisturbed. In a quiet room, sit comfortably, either on the floor (cross-legged or in the lotus position) or on a straight-backed chair.
2. Close your eyes and breathe deeply and rhythmically in through your nose and out through your mouth.

3.   Concentrate on the rhythm of your breathing. Feel your lungs expanding and contracting with each breath. Enjoy the sensuous pleasure.

4.   When you feel relaxed and ready to concentrate, consider the following questions:

     *   What is causing you to suffer?
     *   What is distinctive about your suffering?
     *   When does your suffering occur? (What situation/times?)
     *   Who is involved in the cause of your suffering?
     *   Who is not involved? (Consider carefully all those close to you before dismissing them.)
     *   What is involved in the cause of your suffering? (Which object/situation?)
     *   What is not involved? (Which object/situation?)

Do not feel that you have to answer all the questions in one session. You can repeat the meditation until you have considered them all. You may wish to write down your answers at different times and compare them for contradictions. In this way you will increase your understanding of the cause of your suffering, so that you can better deal with it.

APPENDIX III

THE PROPHECIES OF SANGRATAN

In our last conversation (see Chapter 12), Sangratan explained that the Lessons of Life are a practical guide to living in harmony with all of the natural world, but warned that there would soon come a time when the elements would realign, and the climate would change in response to the new equilibrium. As we no longer live in nature, we are thoughtless about it, and need to apply the Lessons of Life to help us deal with the changes which are coming. He predicted that, over the next few years:

1.   Throughout the world:
 *   Wind patterns will alter causing great climatic problems.
 *   Areas which do not usually suffer drought will have severe water shortages.
 *   Large-scale flooding will take place where flooding does not usually occur.
 *   Wars will be fought over water sources ('precious water').

2.   In India and the countries to the north of India:
 *   Widespread flooding will occur annually in areas not usually prone to flooding.
 *   Thousands of homes will be washed away.
 *   Unusually, even some valleys in the Himalayas will be inundated.
 *   Thousands will die of waterborne diseases.
 *   Large-scale violence will occur as men fight over water and natural resources.
 *   In some areas the soil will be contaminated.
 *   In other areas large-scale subsidence will occur.